THY KINGDOM COME

The New Evolution of the Good

⊕

THY KINGDOM COME

The New Evolution of the Good

⊕

Valentin Tomberg

Angelico Press

First published in German in
Lazarus komm heraus!
as "'Dein Reich Komme': Die Drei Reiche
der Natur, des Menschen und Gottes"
(Third of 4 separate texts) Hrsg. v. Kriele, Martin
© Verlag Herder Basel, Freiburg 1985
First English edition in *Covenant of the Heart*
Element Books, Rockport, MA, 1992
Second English edition, in *Lazarus Come Forth!*
Lindisfarne Books, Gt Barrington, MA 2006
Third English edition (as separate book)
newly-translated, with supplements,
Angelico Press, Brooklyn, NY 2022
English translation © James Wetmore 2022

For information, address:
Angelico Press
169 Monitor St.
Brooklyn, NY 11222
angelicopress.com

ISBN 978-1-62138-837-1 (pbk)
ISBN 978-1-62138-838-8 (cloth)
ISBN 978-1-62138-839-5 (ebook)

Cover Design: Michael Schrauzer

TABLE OF CONTENTS

Foreword

I N HIS FINAL YEARS, VALENTIN TOMBERG WROTE four short works, which, after his death, were published together in German as *Lazarus komm heraus!*[1] The present book, the first of these late works (c. 1967), here published separately, was dedicated to his son Alex. The second and longest of the four (1970), *Lazarus: The Miracle of Resurrection in World History*, has been published by Angelico Press. The third in the series, *The Proclamation on Sinai: Covenant and Commandments*, was finished in 1972. A final essay, begun during this period but left unfinished, is included in the present book under the title "The Living Spirit-Breath: A Fragment." These late writings, taken as a whole, may be seen as a "resurrection" of Tomberg's "Our Father Course," given in the Netherlands (1940–1943), which elucidates in an astonishingly profound way the seven petitions of the Our Father prayer. For this reason, an excellent way to summarize and "situate" these last writings is to bring them into relation, text-by-text, with the theme of the seven petitions.

---

[1] Basel: Herder Verlag, 1985. In an earlier English translation, this text was published first as *Covenant of the Heart: Meditations of a Christian Hermeticist on the Mysteries of Tradition* (Rockport, MA: Element, 1992), and again later as *Lazarus Come Forth!* (Gt Barrington, MA: Lindisfarne Books, 2006).

The present work, *Thy Kingdom Come: The New Evolution of the Good,* is clearly a meditation on the SECOND PETITION: "Thy kingdom come." *Lazarus: The Miracle of Resurrection in World History,* which depicts, among other things, the intercessions or irruptions of Christ's healing miracles into world history, may be seen as a further meditation on the THIRD PETITION: "Thy will be done, on earth as it is in heaven." *The Proclamation on Sinai: Covenant and Commandments* is largely a study of the ten names of God, and thus a further meditation on the FIRST PETITION: "Hallowed be thy name." As for "The Living Spirit-Breath: A Fragment," it marks the beginning of an extended, but unfinished, meditation on the FOURTH PETITION: "Give us this day our daily bread." Here, "bread" is expanded into a symbol for nourishment as a whole, which, in its primal form as *Ruach Elohim,* can be called "breath," understood as spiritual, soul, and bodily nourishment: *panem supersubstantialem.* In this very last of his writings, Tomberg reaches back all the way to his very first intimation as a small child of the presence of God in the world, which he movingly recalls in its introduction.

We are most fortunate that these precious works, these "resurrections" of the worthy gleanings of Tomberg's personal path of destiny during the twilight of his earthly life, are being made available in this time of pitched conflict between the powers of good and evil. Our guiding hope in presenting this series is that some readers may resolve to take up the thread of Tomberg's life-mission, for clearly the last work in this series ended abruptly. What if we were to take further his interrupted meditations on "breath" and "bread"? What if we were to ponder further, in the same spirit, in solitude or in community, the fifth, sixth, and seventh petitions of the Our Father Prayer, for which he left no corresponding final meditations?

When considering the course of our own lives, we might well ask: What in *my* past is worthy of resurrection? And as for the worthy gleanings granted me in my earthly life, have I offered these up to the resurrecting power of Christ and thus to the "Church" in its fullest sense as the *Ecclesia universalis*? Let us, then, widen our vision so that we also may hear ringing, throughout all times and in all places, the resounding call: *Lazarus, Come Forth!*

The Three Kingdoms[2]

In the present study, *Thy Kingdom Come*, regarding the kingdom of nature, the kingdom of man, and the kingdom of God, written in the winter of 1966–1967, Tomberg is concerned (as in his contemporaneous magnum opus *Meditations on the Tarot: A Journey into Christian Hermeticism*) with leading readers into the strata of a deeper reality.

The Kingdom of Nature. That path leads first of all through knowledge of the kingdom of nature, which (as we soon learn) can be looked at from two points of view.

Firstly, nature for the Darwinian is a process of evolution determined by the struggle for existence, the survival of the fittest, and natural selection. Tomberg describes this Darwinian nature as the "fallen" nature of the serpent—the serpent, whose guiding principle may be summarized as "the collective will to power." The serpent is endowed with clev-

---

[2] This summary has been condensed from a presentation provided by Tomberg scholar Michael Frensch in *Valentin Tomberg: Leben–Werk–Wirkung*, Bd. I.2 (Schaffhausen: Novalis Verlag, 2005), 470–73.

erness and cunning "as the sum-total of experience offered by evolution and by its earthbound realism." But make no mistake: the serpent is necessary as regards the process of evolution, which is why it is not denied by the Bible. Destiny has allocated the serpent a place:

> "Upon your belly you shall go, and dust you shall eat all the days of your life." (Genesis 3:14) To this latter corresponds the serpent's cunning, its earthly realism, moving horizontally in time from one experience to the next, never raising itself up, ever "going on its belly" and nourishing itself on "dust"—on the dividing-up and analytic splintering of the totality of the world of appearances into ever smaller pieces, as atoms, electrons, particles, etc. To earthbound realism, "knowledge" means dissecting things to ascertain how they are joined together in the larger whole: this is "eating dust." The essence of the serpent's cunning is most comprehensively revealed in empirical, materialistic science, where it has blossomed. [11]

Secondly, in considering the kingdom of nature we also indisputably observe "a remarkable degree of cooperation, association, and social collectivism." [5] For instance, most predators are peaceful and playful in their adolescence, as if pointing to a state prior to or higher than nature insofar as it has evolved in the Darwinian sense—as if pointing, that is, to a region of *created* beings rather than to an "origin of species" driven entirely by *evolution*. For instance, other predators, such as reptiles, who display their cunning, clever, "will-to-power" nature right from their birth, seem by contrast to be products of evolution pure and simple. This key distinction between creation and evolution eludes science because it is blinkered by its own handicaps and rules. Today, however, it is becoming ever clearer that scientific progress (above all, scientific progress when operating without a code of ethics) is leading not only to an ever accelerating "separation and splitting of the whole," but is threatening the very survival of the earth and the plurality of species.

The Kingdom of Man. Are we permitted to do everything we "can" do (according to the serpent's teaching of the "will-to-power")? This question brings Tomberg to the human situation in general, that is, to the kingdom of man. It can be readily seen that we are not merely "products of evolution" (or "children of the serpent"), for we also raise ourselves to a higher order. As we have progressed from the first sacrificial stone altars to lofty cultural creations, philosophical ideas, and profound religious interiority, this life in a higher order has come ever more clearly into view. In contrast to all other creatures of the earth, we as human beings are in a position to raise ourselves above evolution. Our understanding confesses itself as appertaining to a higher world order: by our own efforts, we become capable of *contemplation.*

> Through the capacities of our deeper nature, we have wrenched reason away from natural evolution. That is, to the degree to which reason is conducive to pure contemplation, we have treated it as a kind of booty. Contemplation is the condition of the mind when concentrated on transcendental concepts, ideas, and ideals—and *not* on utility and advantage, as in the case of materialistic realism. It thereby sets itself in harmony with our divine-archetypal nature and becomes a creative fountainhead of things that, as

regards the diversity of natural evolution, are not
only unnecessary or lacking in utility, but are often
downright impediments to survival in the usual sense!
[...] Such is the kingdom of man, situated between
the kingdom of nature and the kingdom of God. Sovereignty of the contemplative mind *together with the
morality it gives rise to*: this is the "pure humanism"
that stands between nature and God. [19–20, 23]

It is in precisely this "pure humanism" that the kingdom of
man manifests itself.

The Kingdom of God. We human beings, however, are called
to raise ourselves up not only out of the kingdom of nature,
but also out of the higher order of the "pure humanism" of
the kingdom of man, to the *kingdom of God.*

As a source of guidance, we may say that the Sermon on
the Mount informs us of our true nature in this respect and
points out our way. Tomberg's treatment and interpretation
of the Sermon on the Mount is highly original in this connection, as for example in considering the second beatitude:
"Blessed are they that mourn, for they shall be comforted."
Now, the goal for advocates of natural evolution is to *banish*
suffering, sickness, and death as far as possible from life, in
order to be happy and without such suffering. But the second beatitude implies that it is in fact precisely *those who
suffer*, "those who mourn," who will find bliss and consola-
tion! If this is so, if true bliss is connected to the experience
of suffering, or mourning, then clearly the absence of suffering is in no way a goal worth striving for:

> For the fullness of existence—life's true richness—is
> not made up of health and happiness only, but of an
> ever-expanding *range* of joy and sorrow; and the

broader the range, the richer life becomes. Goethe said it thus:

> The infinite gods give everything
> To those they love:
> All joys, which are infinite;
> All sorrows, which are infinite.
> These they give wholly.

This richness, this extended range of our capacity for joy and sorrow, reaching up to the divine, is, precisely, blessedness (*beatitudo*). [30–31]

If the watchword of the "old" natural evolution of the serpent was "ye shall be as gods, but without God," then the Sermon on the Mount promises in its stead "ye shall be as God, in God." [29–30] Instead of "indefinitely distancing ourselves from God in the current of natural evolution, we must walk the path of purification, illumination, and perfection (union)." [46]

When and if humanity shall at last have understood this rightly, there will, according to Tomberg, be a new historiography, written by a new breed of historians who will tell first of temptations, deserts, errors, and the way of purification. Such historians

> will trace the deepening insights we have gained by overcoming these temptations, how these advances first shone forth, and what manifold forms they assumed. Their purpose in all this will be to record our progress on the way of illumination. Finally, these historians, these scribes of our spiritual history, will tell the stories of specific individuals and groups who have served as pathfinders on the way to unitive perfection. They will tell, that is, of those whose qual-

ities and capacities have borne witness that the kingdom of man *can* unite and commingle with the kingdom of God. [48]

It remains to say only that, although this study of the Three Kingdoms is distinguished by a great wealth of references to other cultures and their mysteries, the Bible provides its essential point of reference.

Publisher's Note

VALENTIN TOMBERG MAKES UNUSUAL DEMANDS on his readers in terms both of content and of the spectrum of traditions, perspectives, and vocabularies he adopted over the course of his life. This means that, as regards any given book, some readers will be more familiar than others with its conceptual terrain: Anthroposophic, Hermetic, Jurisprudential, or Ecclesial.[1] Unless otherwise noted, footnotes are from the editor/translator. We acknowledge with warm thanks Joel M. Park and Michael Frensch, to whom the first and second parts of the Foreword, respectively, owe their guiding threads, and Richard Bloedon for his editorial scrutiny (together with his colleagues Claudia McLaren Lainson and Brian Wolff). A special thanks goes to an expanding circle of friends and supporters whose shared conviction of the pivotal importance of Tomberg's work has been a constant encouragement.

JAMES R WETMORE

---

[1] One might also say "Catholic" (in the sense of the Roman Catholic Church) with the proviso that it be taken in the extended sense of a truly Universal Church ("catholic" *means* "universal"), or *Ecclesia universalis*. Tomberg does not employ this latter term; we propose it solely for the sake of a clear distinction.

I

The Kingdom of Nature

Introduction

VER SINCE THE APPEARANCE OF CHARLES DAR-
win's theory of the natural evolution of species,
the convictions of anyone with even a modicum
of education have undergone radical change.
Nature has not only come to be regarded primarily as an
object of research and exploitation to be altered and shaped
to our use, but is increasingly deferred to as the sole source
from which we might hope to discover the meaning of life,
its goal, and even the foundations of morality! What the
Bible meant for Europeans of former days has been superseded by the implications of viewing nature *as caught in the
grip of evolution.* This nature—conceived as evolving—is
not the nature our forebears marveled at as God's Creation:
to their wondering, probing, poetic gaze, nature appeared
as a finished work. Nowadays, however, most regard nature
as a *process,* a ceaseless becoming, and not at all as a perfected work. We are led to believe by such people that what
we observe in nature are labor pangs pointing to a *future* we
cannot even imagine, a future in which nothing will be left
of what we now know as nature—including even ourselves!
We are to believe that the glory and perfection of nature lie,
not in her origin and past, but in her future. To be a devout
evolutionist (and who is not these days?) means to believe

1

in the future, and to deem inferior anything of the past. It means to believe in a wretched, soulless, spiritless past—somehow sprung from a blind, whirling mass of primeval gas—and in a brilliant future to be shaped and dominated by the reasoning faculty ramped up to a degree that we cannot presently conceive.

If nature really did evolve plants, animals, and man (not forgetting the poets and sages among us!) from a vortex of gas, why should we not turn to her (and only her) for instruction on the meaning of life and guidelines of right aspiration, thinking, and behavior? Where better than from nature (that is, from life itself) could we hope to learn the real what, why, and how of life? And all the more so, if we believe ourselves to be no more than fragments of nature somehow grown fit for self-reflection!

Untold numbers of our contemporaries think in just this way, and consider it their bounden duty to apply lessons learned from nature as guiding principles for all their undertakings.

Nature's Teaching

The natural sciences have placed a great mass of factual information at our disposal—from which, by analysis, it has proven possible to draw general conclusions that we might call "nature's teachings." These teachings have been inferred from the scientific data in the same way evidentiary conclusions in jurisprudence are inferred from careful review of the facts of any given case. But even so, nature *herself* is not in the business of drawing conclusions about herself! Nature doesn't teach; she simply acts. Or perhaps better said, simply "happens." We cannot deny, however, the significance of the implications of nature's happenings, which can speak volumes. For instance, the fact that dinosaurs once ruled the earth but then disappeared, giving way to weaker but more adaptable mammals, is a happening in nature which teaches us that highly specialized creatures (those capable of realizing the highest degree of development in some particular niche) are the least suited to further development, whereas less specialized creatures (those better able to adapt)—although often weaker—are better able to survive and develop further, owing to their more generalized capacities. That is, the one-sided development of a highly specialized creature proves to be an evolutionary dead end: it reaches the highest level of attainment (the "world record" so to speak) in some particular direction, but by this same token forfeits the possibility of further development in any other direction. Since such a creature has need precisely of alternative directions of development in order to survive amid ever-changing conditions by keeping step with the onward march of evolution, it perishes. The extinction of the dinosaurs, then, brings to light nature's teaching that specialization is a blind alley and spells ruin, whereas adaptability portends life and progress.

As regards the continued existence or the extinction of a species and the preservation or destruction of an individual within a species, the decisive factor is that the "fit" are worth saving and the weak expendable and soon to perish. For example, the battling of stags in rutting season establishes which among them are most fit and hence most deserving of siring young. And just as the struggle for survival determines which individuals within a species endure and which are rejected, so also do species as a whole struggle for existence in the natural world.

We are told that there is afoot in nature a will to power, whose self-assertive goal is its own survival, as though nature were engaged in conjuring a prodigious creature adapted to meeting every challenge and overpowering every opponent—directing all its effort to producing this prodigy!

Could this prodigy be man? "Not yet," answered Friedrich Nietzsche. Man is only a stepping-stone on the way to this being. In the end, man will be superseded in order that nature's prodigious conjuration, the superman (*Übermensch*), may be realized. For if man is that part of nature which has thus far become self-conscious, the superman (or, "the one who is coming") will not only be nature grown *self-conscious,* but nature grown *self-willed.* Should this actually come to pass, the Delphic Oracle, "Man, know thyself," would be replaced by the Will Oracle, "Man, will thyself"—for the crown of natural evolution would then no longer be self-reflection, but self-actualization. Such "coming-ones" would not merely recognize and acknowledge freedom, but actually *be autonomous.* Their will power would be an inexhaustible font of creativity untrammeled and unconditioned by anything other than itself.

"O Thou my Will, my Necessity, my Law!" Such was Nietzsche's prophetic cry, for he was himself well advanced on the path toward the secret of the will that operates in the evolutionary processes of nature, slithering upward through the mutating forms of nature's successive kingdoms until it achieves consciousness and autonomy. It is the will below which smolders in the persuasive, compelling promise: "Ye shall be as gods!"

Nature's Other Teaching

But wait. What happens in nature attests not only to a struggle for existence assiduously selecting those fit to survive. It attests also to a remarkable degree of cooperation, association, and social collectivism. Anthill and termite colony, wasp nest and beehive, wolf pack and elephant herd (indeed, every living organism whose cells work together, every molecule of a healthy cell, every atom with its system of electrons) are examples of cooperation, association, and social collectivism in nature. Electrons unite in atoms, atoms in molecules, molecules in cells, cells in organisms. Organisms in turn work together in colonies, communities, herds, tribes, races, nations, governments, and confederations.

The late prime minister of South Africa, General Smuts, was so struck by nature's collective activity that he not only elaborated a philosophy of holism (from the Greek *holon* = totality) but also, on holistic grounds, aligned his country with the British Commonwealth. It was for this reason that, not only in time of peace but through both World Wars, South Africa remained a faithful member of the Commonwealth, with all the obligations this entailed.

But General Smuts was not the only one in recent times so impressed by a comprehensive view of nature's integrative processes that he sought to apply them on the sociopolitical level. Over half a century earlier, Karl Marx and Friedrich Engels had been entranced by the spectacle of the struggle for existence in nature and how, by alliance in groups and collectivities, the weaker amassed strength. Marx and Engels unleashed upon mankind the impassioned plea: "Workers of the world, unite!" Their call to

5

those oppressed in life's struggle for existence (a struggle that also plays out in human society) was a call to unite and take joint action against oppressors in the higher echelons, to shake off their rule, to replace competition and rivalry with a new, worldwide social order founded on cooperation. They believed that such a communal society should have as little to do with exploiters and the exploited as does an ant colony, where no individual exploits or enslaves another, but each serves as part of the whole, never claiming a position of power or privilege for itself.

To the thinking of Marx and Engels, what is instinctively realized in a colony of ants should be achievable in a communal society through reasoned conviction. They regarded *reason* as instinct-grown-conscious, *instinct* as the categorical expression of the essential nature of the matter that constitutes all things, and *matter* as in turn inhabited by a primal instinct destined one day to rise resplendent, illuminating all things to our (by then) fully-evolved faculty of reason as a prodigious all-embracing fund of knowledge.

What is this primal instinct? It is the urge for progress: progress not only for the few or the elect, but for all. And is not precisely this instinct for progress what smolders in the depths of evolution's promise: "*Ye* shall be as gods!"? Note well: the promise is not "*you* or *he* or *she* shall be as a god." "Being as gods" is the concern of mankind as a whole—and as such, according to this view, it represents its collective goal.

The Serpent's Cunning

If we now broaden our focus, we may equally well take the natural-scientific conception of evolution in its entirety as *itself* a single, large-scale happening in nature. If we do this, we discover that *its* teaching is pointing to an indefatigable driving force active in the depths of all becoming. It is a force that adopts, then discards, myriad forms—striving always to rise from dark instinct to the clear light of reason. Understood in this sense, evolution is *synonymous* with instinct striving to become reason.

This process does not proceed in a straightforward way, but by trial and error. It tests and probes, takes byways, wanders down blind alleys. When it does these things, it is seeking a way out in order to resume its primary direction. It follows a winding path, like the track of a serpent slithering through darkness. Nonetheless, that track *does* indicate a general direction in which the movement takes place, one progressing toward organic forms capable of reason.

⊕

It may be instructive at this point to note the peculiar role indigenous peoples (and others also) have attributed to the *serpent*. Several years ago (in the 1960s), the British television network broadcast the first documentary of the rites of the Australian aborigines. It was produced and narrated by David Attenborough, a depth-psychologist with a special interest in the "mysteries" of so-called primitive peoples. The aborigines made an exception in the case of this congenial and sympathetic man, according him the high honor of allowing him to attend their rites. Nor did he betray their trust, for the film he produced as a result offered profound insights that could not do otherwise than awaken in the viewer respect for the childlike gravity with which this small group of our fellowmen, poor and naked though they were, enacted in deepest reverence what they hold most sacred. The primary rite, a presentation in dramatic form of their central tradition, was intended to evoke the primordial memory subsisting in their subconscious *of the origin and evolution of consciousness.* A man, evidently in a trance in which he had identified himself with a serpent, crept out through a cleft in a rock and, swaying rhythmically, slowly approached a group of his fellows in the foreground. Upon reaching them, he emerged from the trance and collapsed, after which he came to himself and rose up as a man among men. At the back of the grotto, a slab of wood, inscribed with symbols, depicted the serpent's journey from the dark depths of matter to the stature of man. This wooden "book" of symbols was then displayed to all present.

In her major opus, *The Secret Doctrine*, H.P. Blavatsky presented many Indian and Tibetan traditions concerning the serpent and the "sons of the serpent." These traditions show that in those regions the serpent was regarded as the originator and teacher of civilization, of the arts and sciences, of invention and the use of tools. The message of these traditions was that the *nagas,* or "sons of the serpent," were mankind's first teachers—that the serpent was the principle of intellectual and material progress.

For their part, the gnostic sects of the Naasenes (from *naas* or *nahash* = serpent in Hebrew) and the Ophites (from *ophis* = serpent in Greek) worshipped the serpent as the cosmic principle of progress. They took as their symbol the serpent swallowing its tail, the same chosen by the Theosophical Society as its seal and standard.

⊕

The Bible, however, does *not* ascribe to the serpent the role of human benefactor, but that of tempter and malefactor. The serpent as presented in the Bible effected the most radical alteration imaginable in the existential conditions and destiny of mankind: the Fall from the condition of Being, or the realm of divine archetypes (the garden of Eden planted by God), into that of evolution—that is, a world (directed by the serpent) that seeks by means of toil, suffering, and death to attain its stated end: "Ye shall be as gods!" Friedrich Weinreb writes in his important work *Roots of the Bible*:

> The serpent has something to offer to man. The serpent is the physical Messiah, one might say. It offers the kingdom of this world, the kingdom of endless development.[1]

Such a kingdom is one evolving toward fully automatic (hence, *godless*) consciousness—a consciousness "like unto God and, consequently, in no need of Him."

> It has been pointed out that the word for serpent in Hebrew, *nahash*, spelled 50-8-300, has as its total 358 [nun = 50, heth = 8, shin = 300]. And that is also the sum-total of the components of the word Messiah [*masiah*], spelled 40-300-10-8 [mem, shin, yod, heth]. So, serpent and Messiah have the same sum-total of components. . . . The serpent is the Redeemer on the opposite side, [who] proposes emancipation in advis-

---

[1] Friedrich Weinreb, *Roots of the Bible: An Ancient View for a New Vision* (Brooklyn, NY: Angelico Press, 2021), 94.

ing to set to work oneself, to take development in one's own hands. . . . *That* is the serpent's subtlety, that it acts as the Redeemer.[2]

The Bible and the people of Israel performed an inestimable service by exposing evolution as the work of the serpent, by unmasking it as teacher of a path leading further and further away from God, and from man's true home. The serpent is venerated (whether expressly or not) wherever evolution is taken to be the guiding power of the natural world in which all take part, whereas the Bible stands alone in warning of the serpent's path and recalling the supra-evolutionary homeland and destiny of mankind.

Continuing on from the Old Testament, the gospels speak of the "sons of this world" and the "sons of light." (Luke 16:8) The former are the "peoples" (*gentes,* usually translated "the heathen"); the latter are those dedicated to serving God, and not the "Lord of this world"—the serpent, or guiding being of evolution. The sons of light understand that evolution is the path of the serpent, which causes so many to "go astray."

> The word lose or lost ["go astray"] in Hebrew is *abed,* spelled 1-2-4 [aleph, beth, daleth]. It has in its structure the development from the "one" to the "two," but instead of the return to the "one" there is the further development of the "two" to its highest perfection, the "four." Now this development is identical with "getting lost" ["going astray"].[3]

---

[2] Ibid., 94–95.
[3] Ibid., 95.

It is written in the gospels that the "sons of this world" are wiser, after their fashion, than are the "sons of light." (Luke 16:8) The comparison being drawn here is between the wisdom of the divine light and the cunning of the serpent. Indeed, this cunning—taken as the sum-total of experience offered by evolution and by its earthbound realism—undoubtedly *does* exist and *is* valid with respect to the evolutionary realm. This is why the gospels do not deny it but *validate* it, in its proper domain: "so be wise as serpents and innocent as doves" (Matthew 10:16) was the Master's counsel to his disciples. But there is a correlative divine decree in the Old Testament concerning the serpent: "upon your belly you shall go, and dust you shall eat all the days of your life." (Genesis 3:14) To this latter corresponds the serpent's cunning, its earthly realism, moving horizontally in time from one experience to the next, never raising itself up, ever "going on its belly" and nourishing itself on "dust"—on the dividing-up and analytic splintering of the totality of the world of appearances into ever smaller pieces, as atoms, electrons, particles, etc. To earthbound realism, "knowledge" means dissecting things to ascertain how they are joined together in the larger whole: this is "eating dust."

The essence of the serpent's cunning is most comprehensively revealed in empirical, materialistic science, where it has blossomed. Furthermore, the collectivism that makes use of the results of this science (that is, where science "becomes flesh") represents the unfolding of the "morality" of the serpent—a morality rooted in the promise "Ye shall be as gods!" This serpentine morality aspires to unbounded collective progress in the conquest, utilization, and control of the world by a collectively systematized rationality. The essence of the morality of the serpent—the morality of evolution—is the collective will to power, extended directly into the "natural" evolution of mankind.

The Other Side of Nature

Nature in the grip of an evolutionary process (i.e., that nature which modern science has uncovered and investigated) is not, however, the whole of nature. Admittedly, it is the greater part, but nonetheless *only a part*. Another part, *not* caught up in evolution, is generally disregarded because it fails to conform to the evolutionary view—and so is of no interest to those laboring under its spell. Evolution, as currently understood, does not encompass all of nature. This fact is made clear from a simple query: If the mineral kingdom actually did evolve into the plant kingdom, the plant kingdom into the animal kingdom, and the animal kingdom into the human kingdom, why does a mineral kingdom still exist alongside the plant kingdom, a plant kingdom alongside the animal kingdom, and an animal kingdom alongside the human kingdom? Why is it that the greater part of nature has *not* progressed, *even though* it has been situated in the same terrestrial conditions all along?

It is no use looking to some analogy with our human organism for help with this conundrum, for we certainly do not find evidence in our own case that we as human beings set out at the beginning with a mineral skeleton to which, then, by "evolutionary" stages, was somehow appended tendons, muscles, veins, arteries, etc., and finally a cerebral and nervous system—such as we must expect to have happened, were there in fact an *actual* correspondence between our human organism and the evolutionary scheme. No, quite the contrary: by division of a *single* reproductive cell, not only do brain and nerve cells arise, but also those of tendons, muscles, veins, arteries, and bones!

The original cell *differentiates* into the various "kingdoms" within the organism. This is a process corresponding far more to the biblical principle "each according to its kind" than to the principle of "progressive" evolution—by which latter is meant development of the mineral into the organic, and of the organic into a nervous system capable of mediating psyche (or, soul). If ontogenesis is an accelerated recapitulation of phylogenesis, the correct conclusion to be drawn by analogy with the microcosm of the human organism would be that the macrocosm is not solely the outcome of an evolutionary process but (and *primarily*) the product of a process of differentiation also. This means that it was from one single primal substance (whether "primeval gas" or not) that not only the mineral but also the plant and animal kingdoms entered into manifestation *at the same time* in conformity with the biblical maxim "each according to its kind."

Nature has two sides: it is the arena of active manifestation, where the archetypes of the various species appear according to the biblical (and Platonic) maxim "each according to its kind"; and it is also the arena of evolution, where the struggle for existence (the survival of the fittest and natural selection) is played out. The first nature, that of the reflection and incorporation of the archetypes, is *primary*; the second nature, that of "natural" evolution, is *secondary*.

The solar system with its sun and orbiting planets; the atom with its nucleus and electron cloud; the living cell with its center surrounded by a moving plasma of molecules: *none* of these are arenas of the struggle for existence, and still less for evolution, which is in any case valid only for a portion of nature as manifested at the earth's surface. No, these three (solar system, atom, living cell) are structural forms expressing an *archetype*—or what Goethe called a "primal phenomenon" (*Urphänomen*). And if the most all-encompassing of these three (the solar system) as well as the least (atom and cell) manifest one and the same structural archetype, why should there not be further manifestations, situated between these extreme limits, of still other structural archetypes or primal phenomena? Was Goethe mistaken in describing the primal phenomenon or structural archetype of plants—that is, the *prototype* underlying the various species of plants (and thus constituting the theme of which all plant species are only variations)?

An overall view of the world discloses an edifice whose pillars are the archetypes, around which evolution wends its way, adapting, readapting, varying them in diverse ways, in conformity with ends that *it*—and not the world of archetypes—has in view. Evolution proper actually made a late appearance, *after* the process of differentiation had already formed the world into a cosmic organism that could furnish "natural evolution" a stage on which to act. Evolution is not primary and primordial, but secondary, superadded, superimposed. It *begins* its work in the organic realm, initially in a limited way in the plant kingdom, and gains purchase thereby to determine in ever-increasing measure the fate of the animal kingdom and the kingdom of man. In other words, within the biblical (and Platonic) Creation there appeared an evolutionary process that might be called the generation of *another world within the world of Creation*—a world "for itself" that, like a parasite, took root and proliferated throughout the true, actual world-organism.

There is thus both a "virgin" nature and a "fallen" nature. Virgin nature is that of the divine archetypes, bearing paradise within. Fallen nature, having been caught in the clutches of evolution, refashions and modifies these archetypes according to its own designs.

The fact that, in its origin, nature was archetypal (or, paradisal)—and only later fell into the realm of serpent-guided evolution—is also evident from the predatory characteristics of many creatures, which only appear *after* a "paradisal" infancy. It is a case here again, at least in a general sense, of ontogeny recapitulating phylogeny. For instance, lion cubs begin life as cute, friendly creatures no less tame or trusting than lambs, only to mature rather abruptly into predators. The same could be said of many other beasts of prey. However, this does not apply in the case of reptiles. Juvenile snakes and crocodiles are as though fully mature from the start. We cannot avoid the impression that such reptilian creatures originated on "this side" of the threshold of evolution, that the history of these species cannot be divided into distinct "pre-evolutionary" and "evolutionary" periods. They are, so to speak, "pure" products of evolution, for they are *wholly* the serpent's work. The serpent is their creator. Similar remarks could be made regarding many species of insects also.

But where in all this do we as mankind stand?

II

The Kingdom of Man

ROM AN EVOLUTIONARY POINT OF VIEW, MAN presently holds pride of place. For if it is evolution's purpose to lead primal instinct (the serpent's cunning) to the point of self-awareness, there can be no doubt that we are the creatures in whom this purpose has been realized: we are certainly the least instinctive and most intelligent beings yet to appear in the arena of evolution. It was by virtue of our intelligence and our skill with tools that we wrested dominion over the earth from the great beasts of the past.

In us, the will to power (the impelling force behind all evolutionary processes) has attained its highest level yet. Our sovereignty is undisputed; no rivals remain. Our toolmaking (through which we have come to dominate nature) has advanced from stone ax to interplanetary spaceship, from hand spear to hydrogen bomb. But all the same, these attainments represent nothing more than various stages along the way to our conquest and control of nature by sense-bound reason. They share in common that they are achievements of intelligence applied to the acquisition of power by means of perfecting the design and use of tools. But all such attainments, no matter how remarkable they may be, nevertheless *lie on the same plane*—that of the struggle for existence and the will to power. They are merely intellectual prolongations of the instinctual behavior of animals. No essential moral distinction is to be made between the behavior of an ape hurling a coconut at a passerby and that of the pilot who dropped the atomic bomb on Hiroshima. Such differences are solely a matter of the level of technology deployed. The sum-total of all technological development, together with the research in mathematics, chemistry, and physics upon which it rests, is no more than a further extension of "natural evolution" by mankind—the only difference being that it is guided now by reason rather than by instinct.

If we were nothing more than products of natural evolution, we would be living exclusively in the arena of the will to power—and would thereby persist in applying all our faculties to further empowering ourselves. We would be immersed in the horizontally ramifying evolutionary stream of the serpent, to whom we would be joined for all eternity. But a miracle occurred: while flowing with the current of "progress," immersed in empirical and materialistic realism, we raised ourselves up from the plane of natural evolution and its so-called realism: an *idealism* having nothing whatsoever to do with empiricism lit up in us! This happened long before the historical appearance of Platonism and Stoicism, or of Vedanta and Buddhism. In archetype, it happened when, in the far distant past, someone for the first time erected an altar of unhewn stone. All else—the great religions and the totality of idealist philosophies besides—followed upon the erection of that first altar, an act that would have the most far-reaching consequences imaginable, for it was "vertically" opposed to evolutionary processes. It was situated neither on a level with, nor oriented in the direction of, empirical-materialistic realism.

To what does this miracle of idealism, bursting like a comet into the world of evolution, attest? To our nobility, to the reality that in our deeper being we are no mere product of natural evolution, to the fact that the world of natural evolution only points to (but actually *is not*) our true nature or spiritual home.

That first stone altar offers irrefutable proof that we professed therewith our allegiance to a cosmic order *other* than that of natural evolution; for in its design, it offered neither a weapon for survival nor shelter from storm or foe. Kant's well-known twin sources of wonder ("the starry heaven above and the moral law within") express clearly what the first altar-builder mutely professed through the telltale fact of erecting his altar. For the "starry heaven above" is an image of divine-archetypal nature, not the nature under the sway of natural evolution; and the "moral law within" (Kant's "categorical imperative") signifies the reality of the presence in us of what the Bible calls the "image and likeness of God," which is no other than our divine archetype.

The miracle of idealism, of our rising up from the meandering current of natural evolution, is that we do not merely *postulate* a world order and a morality other than those of the serpent, but that, in so doing, we *employ* the very faculties whose development we *owe* to the serpent (reason and its attendant senses) *against* the purposes and ends of this same evolution!

Contemplation. We have elevated reason from its engagement with the use of tools and its dominion over nature (along with its capacity to calculate, establish causality, and achieve the greatest yield with the least effort) to the level of *pure contemplation.* Through the capacities of our deeper nature, we have wrenched reason away from natural evolution. That is, to the degree to which reason is conducive to pure contemplation, we have treated it as a kind of booty.

Contemplation is the condition of the mind when concentrated on transcendental concepts, ideas, and ideals—and *not* on utility and advantage, as in the case of materialistic realism. It thereby sets itself in harmony with our divine-archetypal nature and becomes a creative fountainhead of things that, as regards the diversity of natural evolution, are not only unnecessary or lacking in utility, but are often downright impediments to survival in the usual sense!

We have contemplation to thank for such philosophies as Sankhya, Vedanta, Buddhism, Pythagoreanism, Platonism, Stoicism, and Kantianism. All these idealist philosophies are "strangers to the world"—to the world, that is, of natural evolution. We owe no invention, no new tool, to these philosophies (or at best, perhaps, to a few musical instruments—but then, music is no mark of technological progress *per se*).

Idealism. We have referred to idealist philosophies (and not religions) because they are not only purely human, but have elevated the faculty of *reason* (stemming from natural evolution) to the level of *contemplation*. By contrast, religions cannot be regarded as purely human expressions or creations: their provenance transcends the purely human, for they spring from the font of supra-human, divine revelation. This is why the purely human manifests in idealism, not in divine revelation.

Idealism is where we express our innermost being: it is the "voice of one crying in the wilderness," issuing its call from a place *between* the domains of natural evolution and

20

divine revelation—between the kingdoms of nature and of God. Only in this intermediary place can our *human voice* be heard, in and of itself: not the voice of those dominated and bullied by natural evolution (the "children of this world"), not the voice of enlightened and inspired religious prophets and seers, but our *own* human voice when crying out from the loneliness of our true being. For our true being is not revealed in technological progress (which, as we have seen, is only an extension of natural evolution) but in an idealism representing our capacity for contemplation—that is, with no practical end in view.

It is in idealism that we commence being human in the true sense of the word. What is pre-idealistic is pre-human, and belongs to the realm of natural evolution—the realm of the serpent. The morality of those who confess the serpent's realm (empirical-materialist realists) is rooted in utility and expediency, whether on an individual or collective level. By contrast, idealists (those capable of contemplation) possess a morality rooted not in cunning intelligence, but in knowledge of the nobility of man's true nature. Their fundamental rule is self-mastery, mastery by our higher nature of the conditions of the "natural man" in whom we dwell, mastery of the contemplative mind over impulsive and passionate drives.

Human Virtues & Morality. This explains why Plato regarded intellectual discernment (which he called wisdom) as the root and source of all the virtues. In his view, the other virtues (courage, prudence, and justice) follow from the penetration of the whole man by the ever-intensifying light of wisdom. Plato conceived of justice as the ultimate issue of this penetration of the whole man by the light of wisdom. Justice, which for him was nothing other than self-mastery—and thus represented the crown of mankind's moral development—could just as fittingly be called "wisdom become flesh."

The Indian sage Sankaracharya also describes four fundamental virtues in connection with the path of realization. The first, the root-principle of the others, is discernment (*viveka*) between the essential and the non-essential. From this follows equanimity (*vairagya*), which enables the development of the "six jewels": moral habits that, taken together, guarantee conduct governed by prudence in every circumstance. The fourth and last virtue (or, quality) is the aspiration for liberation from the shackles of *nature in the grip of natural evolution*.

For Sankaracharya, as for Plato, it is a matter of establishing the sovereignty of the contemplative mind over all other aspects of our nature. Plato regarded wisdom as the basis for moral growth; Sankaracharya pointed to discernment between the essential and the non-essential (a faculty very similar, of course, to Plato's wisdom) as the basis for that same moral growth. Sankaracharya's equanimity corresponds to Plato's courage, and his "six jewels" taken together are none other than Plato's virtue of prudence. The sole divergence between these two thinkers appears in the final crowning and integrating virtue, which for Plato is justice and for Sankaracharya the aspiration to freedom or liberation.

The morality of Buddhism presented in the Noble Eightfold Path, oriented likewise towards "right meditation" or contemplation, also sets a foundation for the full development of the contemplative mind. And the same can be said of the Stoics, whose morality is one of the sovereignty of the contemplative mind: man's self-mastery through reason.

Such is the kingdom of man, situated between the kingdom of nature and the kingdom of God. Sovereignty of the contemplative mind *together with the morality it gives rise to*: this is the "pure humanism" that stands between nature and God.

III

The Kingdom of God

Salvation in Human History

F WE CONTEMPLATE MANKIND'S HISTORY AS AN episode against the broader background of world evolution, we begin to see it as embedded in a panorama of events extending far beyond not only the realm of natural evolution (including its extension into technology), but beyond even the divine-archetypal realm of virgin nature (including its extension in pure idealist humanism). It is from this further realm beyond the other two that supranatural and suprahuman interventions flow into the affairs of the kingdoms of both nature and man. Taken together, we may call these interventions, representing inflows from the kingdom of God into the course of natural evolution and human history, the history of revelation and the work of salvation. Evolution *as a whole*, then, is made up of natural evolution, of purely human cultural history, and of the history of revelation and the work of salvation.

Natural evolution along with its technological extension stands under the watchword "ye shall be as gods!" It is an unending, ever-widening withdrawal from God as Creator of archetypal nature and archetypal man. From the standpoint of spirituality and morality, it represents the "way of eternal damnation." By "damnation" we mean confinement

25

in the closed circle of the serpent swallowing its own tail—
that is, end-stage imprisonment, even of our consciousness,
in the serpentine but enclosed path of natural evolution,
from which there is no escape. In the context of world history, "hell" is the world of "eternal return," a world "without miracles" that holds out no hope of escape from the
mechanism of causality. Damnation means "being as
gods"... without God!

On the other hand, revelation and the work of salvation,
or salvation history, breaches the circle of damnation or
natural evolution, breaking open the possibility of entry
into and exit from it. Salvation history comes to the aid of
those of an idealist frame of mind who, although having
come far enough to no longer identify with natural evolution, still lack sufficient strength to alter its course away
from eternal damnation. Such people are therefore unable,
on their own, to redirect "the way of the world"—just as
they are unable, on their own, to elevate themselves as did
the famous Baron Münchausen, who reputedly extricated
himself from a swamp by tugging on his own pigtail.

Idealists can at least rise to awareness of their true nature,
and on this basis postulate another world order. But even at
best, this realization amounts to no more than the bare recognition that such a nature really does exist in them.
Beyond this, we may say that, in the course of world history, it is the work of salvation that comes along to offer its
helping hand to lift them higher. Revelation from the
sphere lying beyond that of natural evolution begins to
flow into those who truly yearn for the "beyond."

⊕

Salvation history is thus the history of religion *as revelation.* It is the "hand of God" extended from on high to humanity mired in evolution's stream, in order that we may be raised up and supported in our yearning to make our return to the divine-archetypal world. This helping hand extended by God in answer to our yearning is best expressed in David's psalm:

> Save me, O God,
> for the waters have come up to my neck.
> I sink in the miry depths,
> where there is no foothold.
> I have come into deep waters;
> the flood engulfs me.
> (Psalms 69:1–2)

In answer to this plaintive cry have come successive stages of revelation descending like tumbling cascades, awakening humanity to its divine archetype. This revelatory stream has coursed through seers and prophets and has been recorded and preserved in Holy Scriptures. The revelation vouchsafed to the seven Holy Rishis formed the basis of the Vedas, the Holy Scripture of India. The *Zend-Avesta* of ancient Iran is the record of the revelation communicated to Zoroaster when, from a high mountain refuge, he confronted face to face the God of Light, Ahura Mazda. In its turn, the Bible tells of the revelation received on Mount Sinai by Moses, who encountered, also face to face, the God who bore the ineffable name YHVH.

The primordial revelation of India announced the "good news" (*evangelium*) that divine-archetypal man, man's true self, is not his empirical self; and likewise, that the world, the real or divine-archetypal world, is not the empirical world of natural evolution. The "good news" Zoroaster brought was that the world and mankind are an intermingling of two separate world orders: that of light and that of darkness (that of the divine-archetypal world and that of natural evolution). And further, that the latter would be vanquished in the end by Saoshyant ("who, through will, overcomes death"), after which the resurrection of the dead is to follow. Finally, the "good news" revealed to Moses and the prophets proclaimed that, although having come into the serpent's domain through the Fall, humanity could yet be redeemed. For the very essence and epitome of the divine-archetypal world order Himself was to become Man, so that humanity might triumph over the domain of the serpent—and the dead be resurrected.

Such are the messages of the revelations represented by the great pre-Christian religions. As for Buddhism (rooted, as it is, in Brahmanism), it was not a religious revelation proper, but the culmination of pure humanism. And properly speaking, Confucianism is not a religion either, but a socially and ethically oriented practical philosophy.

If we turn to the post-Christian religions of Mithraism, Manicheanism, and Islam, we can understand them as "renaissances" of Zoroastrianism or Mazdeism (Mithraism), of Buddhism (Manichaeism), and of Mosaic monotheism (Islam).

Each of these religions, these stages of revelation, crystallized into a Law—a system of precepts, or injunctions and prohibitions, framed to regulate the life of the faithful in accord with the content of the particular revelation or divine promise concerned. Now, the moralities of the various religions, and the morality of idealism, have in common a preoccupation with self-control and self-discipline—but with the *difference* that the injunctions and prohibitions implicit in the morality of idealism pertain to the contemplative intellect, whereas those of the religions are not rooted in man's intellect, but in divine revelation. The convincing power of divine revelation does not lie in intellectual *insight* (as is the case with humanistic idealism), but in the *authority* of the revelatory source. It was belief in the authority of this revelatory source that disposed the faithful to comply with the injunctions and prohibitions derived therefrom.

⊕

Now, it happened during salvation history, or the history of religion, that a voice was raised on earth *opposing* natural evolution. It did so not only on the basis of humanity's divine archetype, and not only by pointing to the divine-archetypal world order as against the world of the serpent, but, beyond this, by proclaiming that the kingdom of God had *entered* the realm of human destiny. We find this clearly depicted in the Sermon on the Mount, which is not merely concerned that man preserve his archetypal nature in face of natural evolution, or even that he conform to divinely revealed law, but that, in accordance with his archetype—the image and likeness *of* God—he becomes *as* God. "You, therefore, must be perfect, as your heavenly father is perfect." (Matthew 5:48) This pivotal, epitomizing statement from the Sermon on the Mount is a call to us to ascend, both from the kingdom of nature and from the kingdom of man, to the kingdom of God.

The watchword of the "old" natural evolution was "ye shall be as gods!" but *without God*. As against this, the Sermon on the Mount puts forward its own watchword, which reveals the path leading to the summit of the promise "ye shall be as God, *in God.*"

The Beatitudes

Blessed are the poor in spirit

From the perspective of mankind's spiritual history, the Sermon on the Mount is the counterpart to the temptation by the serpent in paradise, for it promises freedom *with* God, just as the temptation in paradise promised freedom *without* God. It stands, therefore, in complete opposition to the natural evolution of the serpent. The serpent promised a self-sufficient state obviating any need for a God "on high"—insinuating that, in such a state, man's knowledge and power will suffice (that is, they will be "rich"). In contrast to this, the First Beatitude of the Sermon on the Mount proclaims, "Blessed are the poor in spirit, for theirs is the kingdom of heaven." That is, blessed are those who regard as poor any knowledge or power without God, any knowledge or power that is not of God Himself—for they shall partake in the divine-archetypal, creative work of God.

Blessed are those who mourn

Another promise of natural evolution is that the conquest of suffering, sickness, and death will lead to happiness. To this the Second Beatitude responds, "Blessed are those who mourn, for they shall be comforted." Those who mourn or bear sorrow do not strive for an existence free from pain, or turn away from pain; they accept pain. For the fullness of existence—life's true richness—is not made up of health and happiness only, but of an ever-expanding *range* of joy and sorrow: the broader the range, the richer life becomes. Goethe said it thus:

> The infinite gods give everything
> To those they love:
> All joys, which are infinite;
> All sorrows, which are infinite.
> These they give wholly.

This richness, this extended range of our capacity for joy and sorrow, reaching up to the divine, is, precisely, blessedness (*beatitudo*).

Blessed are the meek

Natural evolution is founded on the principle that dominion over the kingdom of nature, and thus over the earth, belongs to those whose will to power is greatest. Such dominion is the preserve of the harsh and unyielding. Rome did not achieve dominion over the Mediterranean region, from Britannia to Mesopotamia and from Germania to Egypt, by befriending their populations and cajoling them over to its side, but by subduing them through the military prowess of its legions! And what holds true of political history holds *equally* true of mankind's expanding dominion over the realms that make up the kingdom of nature: animal, plant, and mineral—and now, as well, the realms of chemical elements, molecules, atoms, and electrons. As against this expansion of power, the new, divinely-directed evolution announced in the Sermon on the Mount offers the countervailing principle, "Blessed are the meek, for they shall inherit the earth."

The realms of the kingdom of nature are to be inherited

31

and ruled by the meek, not by the harsh and unyielding. The power St. Francis of Assisi wielded over birds, fish, and wild wolves was not of a kind any natural scientist, fisherman, forester, or hunter has ever possessed. The same holds true of the obedient service rendered to St. Anthony by hyenas in the Egyptian desert; and for that matter, of many other examples of deference shown by so-called "dumb nature" toward the truly meek. Political life, also, is not wanting in examples where meekness proves the stronger. An example on a global scale where meekness took possession of the "earthly kingdom" (*orbis terrarum*) of its time is that Christianity prevailed in ancient times despite the persecutions it endured. It is an example that cannot simply be explained away. Our own time also offers a convincing example of this in India's liberation from British rule by the non-violent (hence "meek") movement of Mahatma Gandhi, who was inspired by the Sermon on the Mount. Nor can this triumph of meekness be casually written off as "native Indian passivity," or any such thing.

Blessed are those who hunger and thirst for righteousness

The objection routinely raised against renouncing power is that, in doing so, we renounce justice or righteousness also—for whether the injustice we elect to renounce (that is, not resist) is against ourself or against another, in the end we, in effect, grant that injustice free rein. But righteousness is not just a matter of "legal" rights; it is the deep-rooted foundation of our moral life also. In fact, the need for righteousness abides in us with an elemental force to be compared only with hunger and thirst. There is nothing to which children are more sensitive than injustice; nothing wounds them more indelibly than violations of their sense of right and wrong. Any who can recall their childhood know this well, as do any who work with children.

This sense of right and wrong is pronounced among so-called primitive peoples also. The Native Americans were far angrier about the settlers' repeatedly broken treaties than about the lands stolen from them. It was this that led to the majority of the bitter Indian Wars. A tribe assured by treaty that the portion of its lands they had agreed to relinquish would be the last, only to discover some years later that *even what remained to them had also been annexed by settlers*, could not but suffer stifling indignation at this mockery of elementary righteousness. "As is well-known, the natives count for nothing," remarked an embittered Immanuel Kant. Indeed, the Native Americans *did* count for nothing in the eyes of the so-called discoverers of their lands—which was something they could never accept. Their sense of righteousness bristled at the fact that promises were not treated as binding, and that their homeland was regarded as "unoccupied" land, open to outside settlement.

This same sense of righteousness is the primary lever applied by state and party propaganda in so-called civilized societies. Insofar as such manipulation of the sense of righteousness has been perverted to incite revolutions, insurrections, and mass movements, it may be likened rather to a volcanic eruption. But in the end, no such falsely incited uprisings have ever yet *actually* satisfied the hunger and thirst for righteousness. Neither communist nor capitalist social forms have been, or are now, able to satisfy the sense for righteousness. Why? Because they are only variants of the same evil: an industrialism that enslaves and degrades.

It is industrialism, self-created by men after the fashion

of Frankenstein's monster, that has reduced individuals to units of production, qualified at best only to service the operational needs of machines. Whether these machines are the property of the state or of individuals is a matter of indifference. Furthermore, just as no social form can bestow freedom on the individual, so likewise can no social form bestow equality on the individual. For the worker, engineer, factory manager, soldier, officer, and general are not equal. And this remains so, regardless of whether they happen to belong to a communist or a capitalist society. Industrialism brings its own forms of bondage and inequality, just as feudalism did in its time. And how, in any case, would it be possible to banish industrialism from the world—especially at this time of population explosion?

If sought within the domain of natural evolution and its technological extension in human history, righteousness (or freedom and equality) remains an illusion. It is simply not to be found there. Nor will it ever be found there, because the "struggle for survival," translated from natural evolution to the arena of human history, has nothing to do with righteousness. Righteousness must be looked for in an entirely different direction, one that runs perpendicular to the horizontal stream of natural evolution.

Yes, perfect equality and freedom *can* be experienced. They can be experienced when people from all stations of life—rich and poor, young and old—kneel at *holy communion* during the Mass and pray together the well-known formula of self-knowledge and faith in divine mercy: "Lord, I am not worthy to receive you, but only say the word and I shall be healed"—for at *that moment* they are all equal in the divine presence: equal in knowledge of their own imperfections; equal in their profession of the divine perfection. At that moment, true righteousness holds sway, and the hunger and thirst for righteousness is stilled. What is solely of earth, solely of the stream of natural evolution, can never still this hunger and this thirst, for righteousness is a state in which the soul experiences the presence of the supra-earthly, the heavenly.

Blessed are those who are persecuted for righteousness' sake

In considering the Beatitude, "Blessed are those who hunger and thirst for righteousness, for they shall be satisfied," we came to see that it does not refer to some unrealizable earthly equality and freedom, but to the equality and freedom of the state of consciousness called in the Sermon on the Mount the "kingdom of heaven" (*regnum coelorum*). That is, the stilling of this hunger and thirst for righteousness does not entail earthly satisfaction or compensation, but participation in an existential state where there is no *un*righteousness. This is clearly expressed in the further Beatitude, "Blessed are they that are persecuted for righteousness' sake, for theirs is the kingdom of heaven." "Persecution for righteousness' sake" points to unrighteousness that inevitably befalls us in earthly life—although the share in the "kingdom of heaven" we thereby attain serves to reduce such unrighteousness to naught.

Blessed are those . . . who are persecuted falsely on my account

What we have just considered is expressed with even greater precision and significance in the last Beatitude, as given in Luke's gospel: "Blessed are you when men hate you, and when they exclude you and revile you, and cast out your name as evil, on account of the Son of Man! Rejoice in that day, and leap for joy, for behold, your reward is great in heaven. . . ." (Luke 6:22–23) We could wish for no clearer affirmation that the compensatory balance of righteousness lies in the vertical earth–heaven axis, and *not* along the horizontal axis of earthly events. It is the "reward in heaven" that illumines from above the unrighteousness endured in the current of evolution here below, and drives it away like a shadow before the light. This compensatory balance of vertical (or, divine) righteousness is the "reward in heaven." It is the enrichment of *our* human nature, not the punishment of the *perpetrator* of unrighteousness according to the principle of horizontal justice: "An eye for an eye, a tooth for a tooth." (Exodus 21:26)

Furthermore, the righteousness of the "kingdom of God" differs from that expressed in the law of karma as understood in both Eastern and Western esotericism, because its righteousness implies (in full conformity with the principle "an eye for an eye, a tooth for a tooth") that in the further course of earthly events a compensatory balance will be struck. Nevertheless, the karmic form of compensatory balance does at least *imply* atonement rather than punishment, since the conscience-oriented notion of karma is by nature "humanistic." For example, someone who commits an unjust act against another searches out an opportunity (which in good time will assuredly appear, even if in another earthly life) to atone for his unjust act.

Our conscience indeed "hungers and thirsts" for such a law of atonement, rather than one solely of retribution. This law of atonement is, then, *conscience operating in destiny.* This is why karmic determinism must be clearly distinguished from both astrological determinism (the movements of the stars as determining our destiny) and biological determinism (heredity as determining our destiny). Indeed, factors pertaining to conscience (that is, *pre-natal* factors) preside over those both of biological heredity and the natal horoscope. This is why the concept, idea, and ideal of karma belong to a higher level of morality than the legal concept of "righteousness" as retributive justice administered by an external power. The same holds true to an even greater degree with regard to the concepts, ideas, and ideals underlying not only the deterministic principles of astrology and biology, but also those of certain religions—for instance, the teaching of predestination found in both Islam and Calvinistic Christianity.

However, just as the law of karma *morally* surpasses both determinism and retributive justice, so is it surpassed in turn by the law of the righteousness of the "kingdom of God" as expressed in the Sermon on the Mount. For the latter is operative in the most essential realm of all: healing wounds of the heart suffered at the hand of injustice, and transforming the pain of such unjustly inflicted suffering into blessing. At the same time (and without inflicting punishment), it leaves the perpetrators of unjust acts to the tribunal of their *own* conscience, their *own* karma. As *merciful* righteousness, the righteousness of the kingdom of God transcends both the righteousness of retributive justice and the righteousness of atonement (karma). It bestows gifts of eternal value, the light of which causes the shadows cast by the suffering of injustice to vanish!

Blessed are the merciful

All who desire to practice a morality that transcends retribution and atonement—and who actually make the effort—

will have their place in the kingdom of God and His righteousness. Hence: "Blessed are the merciful, for they shall obtain mercy."

The actual *application* of the will (that is, its concrete engagement in the practice of merciful righteousness) is thus a precondition for partaking of the blessings of this righteousness. This fact is made clear not only from the Beatitude just cited, but also from the words that follow immediately after the teaching of the Lord's Prayer. These words (provided in the following quotation) provide a kind of commentary on its fifth petition: "For if you forgive others their trespasses, your heavenly Father also will forgive you; but if you do not forgive others their trespasses, neither will your Father forgive your trespasses." (Matthew 6:14–15)

It is not a desire for the favors and blessings of merciful righteousness that makes one a partaker of this realm and of its righteousness. Rather, it is a desire to put merciful righteousness into actual practice solely *for the sake of* the kingdom of God and His righteousness. "But seek first His kingdom and His righteousness, and all these things shall be yours as well." (Matthew 6:33)

Blessed are the pure in heart

Those who "seek first His kingdom and His righteousness" are the "pure in heart" of the Beatitude "Blessed are the pure in heart, for they shall see God." A pure heart, in the sense of the Sermon on the Mount, is a heart turned away from the realm of natural evolution and its promises, a heart devoted solely to the kingdom of God and His righteousness. To such a heart it may be granted not only to discern God in His works, but also to rise further to a vision of Him *as He is in Himself.*

Were the eye not of the sun,
How could we behold the light?
If God's own might and ours were not as one,
How could His work enchant our sight?

This verse by Goethe conforms with the moral logic underlying the Sermon on the Mount, which promises to the
pure in heart the vision of God—the fruit of which is active
cooperation in bringing the kingdom of God to realization
within the earthly world. Indeed, it is the conversion of
natural evolution into a *new* evolution, an evolution willed
and directed by the divine.

Blessed are the peacemakers

The conversion of natural evolution into *a new evolution of
the good* leads first to replacing the former's guiding principle of struggle for survival with the latter's guiding principle
of making peace. For this reason, it is said in the Sermon on
the Mount that the peacemakers are called the "sons of
God." That is, not only do they *see* God, but they *take up
His work*, just as sons take up and continue the work of
their fathers.[1]

⊕

Considered as a world-historical event, the Sermon on the
Mount marked a turning-point in the evolutionary process,
after which the principle of peace is to gradually replace the

---

[1] For "*sons* of God" some Bible translations have "*children* of God";
but the strict sense is "*sons* of god" (e.g., in the RSV Catholic version). To
better contextualize his point regarding sons and fathers, the reader may
turn to the author's *The Proclamation on Sinai: Covenants and*

principle of strife. The path of a new, transformed evolution, both in the case of individuals and of mankind as a whole, begins with a purification of the impulses, instincts, habits, and customs attached to *natural* evolution. It leads on then to illumination—that is, to insight into the truth, beauty, and goodness of *divine* evolution, which is no other than the kingdom of God and His righteousness. Finally, it culminates in the individual's will, feeling, and thinking coming into union with the will, feeling, and thinking at work in divine evolution. This is what we mean by "salvation history." St. Bonaventure characterized this path—that of purification (*purgatio*), illumination (*illuminatio*), and perfection (*perfectio*)—in the most succinct way possible (*De triplici via*, Prologus, I):

> Purification leads to peace,
> Illumination to truth,
> Perfection to love.
>
> *Purgatio autem ad pacem ducit,*
> *illuminatio ad veritatem,*
> *perfectio ad caritatem.*

Commandments (Angelico Press, 2022), where we read: "Father-love sees in the child an 'heir' to continue his life's work, to fight for the same ideal and to further the same task. Mother-love stays true to the image of the original mother–child bond of the pre-natal period: enveloping, protecting, and sustaining." (94) Or again: "Every living tradition is based upon two forces working together: the sustaining force of *memory* (oriented toward the past) and the force of *hope* (oriented toward the future). The former preserves the past from being forgotten, the latter gives shape to the future as the path toward fulfillment. In other words, the *motherly* principle preserves tradition and the *fatherly* principle guides it toward its future goal." (106–7)

Purification, Illumination, & Union as Humankind's Path to God

As we have seen, human destiny, or human history, is played out simultaneously in three realms, or kingdoms: the kingdom of nature, the kingdom of man, and the kingdom of God. This accounts for the fact that we are at once warriors and hunters, bearers of the gift of reason and conscience, and seekers of God endowed with the capacity for love. Or put another way, we are conquerors of nature (*homo faber*), rational thinkers (*homo sapiens*), and prayerful worshippers (*homo pius*). This is why our history is tripartite, comprising a history of "civilization," a history of "culture," and a history of "religion." The culmination of civilization is found in *technology*; the culmination of culture is found in the treasures of *philosophy*; and the culmination of religion is found in *sanctification*, that is, in bringing the kingdom of God to realization as the kingdom of love.

Since these three kingdoms are intimately interconnected, transitions can occur from one to another. For example, from the practice of their "civilizational" craft of measuring and planning, surveyors and architects came to a knowledge of arithmetic and geometry, which they were then able to apply to *contemplation*—thereby bringing the purely quantitative into connection with the qualitative, or "cultural." For them, numbers came to be principles; and geometric figures, symbols. Pythagoreanism offers an example of this transition from the civilizational to the cultural, or from technology to philosophy. Similarly, there have always been (and still are) transitions from philosophy to "religious" life. For example, the cultural quest of philosophy to apply human reason to *truth* could not do otherwise than come to grips with the *religious* implications of *the fact of death*.

Serving as moral "center of gravity" for all serious philosophy (philosophy not distracted from the quest for truth by secondary issues and quibbling) is the reality that, indeed, life ends in death. The problem of death was of such importance for the ancient philosophies that to *be* a philosopher came to mean, quite literally, to be "one preparing for death." Not only Socrates and the Platonists, but the Stoics, Neoplatonists, and Neopythagoreans lived with the *memento mori* ("be mindful of your approaching death") ever before them. And the same holds true—if not even more so—of the Indian and Buddhist thinkers who crowned dying from the world of natural evolution with the ideal of extinction or *nirvana*.

This focus on the problem of death was bound to lead to a search for practical experience that could provide reliable, first-hand knowledge regarding man's fate beyond death's portal. It was precisely this that constituted the meaning and purpose of the "ancient mysteries." And so, we may say that the ancient mysteries represented the transition from cultural-philosophical life to religious life. In those mysteries (for example, the Orphic and Eleusinian mysteries of Greece and the Osiris-Isis mysteries of Egypt), individuals participated in, and acquired experience of, the religious realm—just as, by turning their reasoning capacity from practical concerns to contemplation, they had made the transition from the civilizational realm to the cultural realm of pure humanism.

What was sought in the ancient mysteries (and, according to ancient testimony, *attained*) was experience of a state analogous to death, together with actual after-death conditions of consciousness described as "resurrection." Jean Marques-Riviere writes:

> We find here again the mysteries of Isis and Osiris, and the initiatic value of the *Book of the Dead*. The holy verses, the rules of conduct, and the practical instruction contained in this Egyptian book—a book treating of the way of the dead, and also, as we established previously, the way of the "living"—are precisely what we rediscover in the temple of Eleusis. And we find them again in the rituals of the Orphic initiation, which contain in fact a burial rite of the same type found in the Egyptian *Book of the Dead*, a rite with which the Orphics had themselves interred. The essentials of the esoteric doctrine are the same for Egypt, Eleusis, and the Orphics: what is revealed and experienced are the mysteries of what lies beyond the portal of death. It is the post-mortem state that the adept experiences.[2]

Victor Magnien assembled a collection of ancient testimonies concerning the Eleusinian mysteries in his book *Les mystères d' Eleusis. Leurs origins, le ritual de leurs initiation,* among which we find the following:

> Blessed are they that while yet on earth have seen these things! When death bears them to the *land of shades*, they that have not known, nor had their part, in the holy "orgies," will suffer a destiny unlike that of those that have. (*Hymn to Demeter*)

And further:

---

[2] Jean Marques-Rivière, *Histoire des doctrines ésotériques*, 71.

> Blessed is he that has seen these things before he
> descends into the caves of the underworld. He knows
> life's end and he knows life's beginning—yea, even
> the gift of Zeus! (Pindar, quoted by Clement of Alex-
> andria, *Stromatis* III, 3)

And again:

> Thrice-blessed are those mortals who, after beholding
> these mysteries, enter hades. They alone can thrive
> therein: for the others, all will be suffering. (Sopho-
> cles, *Fragment*)

Victor Magnien himself conceived the nature of initiation
as follows:

> In point of fact, initiation is similar to death. It is
> man's return to his origin. To be initiated means
> learning how to die—i.e., how to reascend to the
> light. Or put another way, it means to die a symbolic
> death by virtue of which all imperfections are left
> behind. On its journey to life in the material realm,
> the soul descends through several levels. To return to
> its origin, it must reascend through these several
> levels. . . . This is why initiation consists of a
> sequence of steps.[3]

Let us add that, ultimately, these steps can be traced back to
three fundamental states of the soul:

purification (*purgatio*);
illumination (*illuminatio*);
perfection (*perfectio*).

---

[3] Ibid., 98.

Or, put another way:

>laying aside the habits, customs, and instincts
> attached to natural evolution;
>awakening to the reality of the divine world of
> archetypes;
>entering this latter world.

⊕

The stages of purification, illumination, and perfection described by St. Bonaventure are the same as those of the ancient mysteries, inasmuch as each such mystery is concerned (at least in a general sense) with progressing through these same three stages—although, to varying degrees, they differ in content. For example, the way of Christian mysticism described and taught by Bonaventure does not consist in learning to *die* and in utilizing (to this end) the magic of initiatic rites and symbolic acts. Rather, his way consists in learning to *live* and to *love*; that is, in entering the "kingdom of God"—in living *in* and *for* this kingdom even during earthly life.

The initiates of the ancient mysteries underwent a unique, extraordinary, and dramatic experience of "the other side." Christian mystics, by contrast, learn to live on "this side"—that is, in the "kingdom of God that has come." The aim of Christian mystics is not a one-time experience of "the other side" undertaken and achieved in order that, by retaining the memory of that one experience, they might live ever after in the fervent hope of leading a "philosophic" life. Their goal is, rather, to live their daily "this side" lives in perpetual union with the divine, spiritual world.

Furthermore, a distinction is to be made between the "perfection" of Christian mystics and that of *mystery initiates*. The perfection of the mystics—mystical union (*unio mystica*)—is a condition or state of life. The perfection of the mystery initiates is a unique, dramatic experience whereby aspirants are raised to the rank of initiate, or *epopt* (meaning "eyewitness" or "one who has seen"). Epopts live on in the afterglow of what they experienced *once*, whereas mystics who have attained the state of perfection live in a state of *perpetual* communication, union, and, finally, unity with God.

If we would choose the way of "return to God" in preference to indefinitely distancing ourselves from God in the current of natural evolution, we must walk the path of purification, illumination, and perfection (union). In truth, our real—our *true*—history consists precisely in walking this path, for it is this path that leads us on to our final destiny.

⊕

If historians of the future have by then discerned the difference between the way, the truth, and the life (on the one hand), and the stream of natural evolution (on the other), they will not be content any longer with recording solely a history of "civilization" (which can only ever be a tale of technological progress and socio-political strife). Instead, they will trace our course as it moves forward through the stage of purification and the stage of illumination, until finally it reaches the stage of unitive perfection. Their narrative will detail the temptations we have faced and overcome, the examples set us by particular individuals and groups, as well as the igniting of new insights and the awakening of new spiritual faculties among us. Such a history will in a very real sense continue the Bible story, for it will take the concerns of the Bible as its own. It will portray our history at the same level and along the same lines as are found in the Bible. Only then will the full purport of the dogma of the inspiration of the Holy Scriptures be fully grasped. Then, too, answers and solutions will be found to theological controversies over such questions as whether the Scriptures are inspired according to the "letter" or according to the "spirit"; whether, in addition to what is inspired, there are also to be found in the Holy Scriptures "uninspired" (that is, purely human) sayings; whether there are "degrees of inspiration" to be found there, ranging from passages where God speaks directly, to passages depicting no more than eyewitness accounts of outer historical events; whether the Holy Scriptures are essentially symbolic or realistic; whether external objects and events are meant as symbols of spiritual realities; etc.

All these difficult questions regarding the inspiration of the Holy Scriptures will be resolved and laid to rest once a sufficient number among us, with the required vocation and sense of responsibility, have taken upon ourselves the Bible's own concern, so that, in stark contrast to the opposing way of natural evolution, we hold unfailingly in view mankind's *true path* as the essence of history.

Such historians will recount, for example, how "in the wilderness" mankind was thrice tempted: with power ("I will give thee dominion over all the kingdoms of the world and their glory"), with materialism ("command these stones to become loaves of bread"), and with the experimental method ("throw thyself down from the pinnacle of the temple")—to put God to the test. They will recognize and portray many great ideological and socio-political movements as well as epoch-making scientific discoveries and technological achievements as just so many examples of these "temptations in the wilderness," just so many decisive milestones along the way of purification. They will trace the deepening insights we have gained by overcoming these temptations, how these advances first shone forth, and what manifold forms they assumed. Their purpose in all this will be to record our progress on the way of illumination. Finally, these historians, these scribes of our spiritual history, will tell the stories of specific individuals and groups who have served as pathfinders on the way to unitive perfection. They will tell, that is, of those whose qualities and capacities have borne witness that the kingdom of man *can* unite and commingle with the kingdom of God.

IV

The Breath of Life

In Lieu of an Introduction

VEN THE MOST PERFECT AND COMPLEX LIVING forms can be traced back to a single cell or seed. Similarly, the ramifications of spiritual growth can be traced back to a seed experience or seed thought. The author of this fragment is no exception in this respect. To just such a seed he owes his own growth to the heights, breadths, and depths of the many-branched tree of knowledge of God. This seed has grown further throughout his life, enabling him to feel and think his way into many forms of religious life—found in different places and at different times in history. But this capacity had nothing to do with studying comparative religion or contriving a syncretic philosophical system: the author simply tried to inwardly sense and experience whatever might deepen, elevate, and expand that fundamental seed-thought and seed-experience first planted in him as follows:

> One day, sixty-eight years ago, when the author was four years old, he was sitting on a colored carpet playing with building blocks. Through an open window, he could see a cloudless blue sky. The child's mother was sitting in a chair, watching him at play. Suddenly the child looked up and, gazing through the

window at the blue heavens, spontaneously asked his mother: "Where is God? Is he in heaven? Does he float there? Or is he sitting there? Where?"

The child's mother sat up straight and gave the following answer, which has held true for the child ever after: "God is present everywhere. We know that, even though we cannot *see* the air, it penetrates everything— and that it is only thanks to the air that we can live and breathe. In this same way, we live and breath in God. And since it is *in* God that we live and breathe, it is from God and thanks to God that we live."

This answer, so clear and convincing, was like a breath of fresh air that ever after blew away any conundrums on this question, leaving behind always the certainty of God's invisible presence everywhere. And as has been said, this seed-thought was to flourish into the heights and depths and breadths, proving to be the primal seed from which a many-branched tree of insight and faith unfolded over the following decades of the author's life.

The Mystery of the Breath

In searching for the meaning of the mysteries of the breath, we cannot do otherwise than begin by meditating on the deeply significant biblical text:

And YHVH ELOHIM formed man of dust from the earth (*adamah*), and *breathed* into his nostrils the *breath* of life (*neshamah hachayim*), and man became a living being (*nephesh chayah*). (Genesis 2:7)

To begin to fathom the meaning of this text, we first need to understand the concepts and ideas of which it consists. The sequence of the text makes clear that man's creation rests upon two divine acts: first, forming his corporeal nature; then, breathing into it the breath of life.

YHVH ELOHIM formed (*yetzer*) man from the dust (*aphar*) of the earth (*min ha-adamah*). St. Jerome, who translated the Bible into Latin, rendered this as follows: "*Formavit Dominus Deus (YHVH ELOHIM) hominem de limo terrae.*" Here *limus* does not mean dry dust, but rather moist earth, which is more in accordance with the biblical context, since in the same chapter (verse 6) we read: "But a mist went up from the earth and watered the whole face of the ground." It is quite natural, then, in picturing the substance from which man's corporeal nature is formed, to see it *not* as *dust* (which presupposes dryness and drought), but as *moist earth*—that is, as the result of a mist surrounding and penetrating everything.

Luther's translation of this passage was still more radical and concrete: "The Lord God made man from a clump of earth"—which certainly presumes the presence of some moisture. But still, the translation "from the dust of the earth" (which is found in the Septuagint) is not without some foundation, for just what *is* the dust of the earth?

For many centuries, dust was thought to consist of minute particles or "atoms." In the sixteenth century, St. John of the Cross wrote in his work, *The Night of the Spirit and the Night of the Senses*, that light as such is invisible, only becoming visible when particles (as well as larger and smaller objects) offer it resistance on its trajectory. According to this view, the *sun's* rays of light are visible because they fall upon atoms of dust and illumine them. Likewise, the *spirit's* light (which, as such, is dark) becomes visible only when it "falls upon" (that is, illumines, by rendering insight and understanding) such "particular" matters as the problems and riddles of existence.

Given that, for St. John of the Cross, the dust permeating the atmosphere is made up of atoms, might not the same conception underlie the biblical dust (*aphar*)? If so, we would be justified in reading the passage in question to mean that man was formed from the smallest particles or atoms of earth (*adamah*)—which leads us, in turn, to ask what the expression *adamah* means.

According to Jewish esoteric tradition (Kabbalah) there are seven types or regions of "earth": *eretz, adamah, geah, nesiah, tziah, arkoah,* and *thebel* (*Zohar* I, 40a). *Eretz* is used in the sense of "land," whereas in biblical language *adamah* signifies "ground" or "soil." Thus *adamah* refers to earth as a fundamental condition or state, pointing to its *qualitative* aspect. In view of this, the "dust of the earth" may best be understood as atoms or minute particles of earth *with a latent aspiration or vocation* to compose man's body. For *adam* means "man," and *adamah* something like "latent manhood." The expression "dust of the earth" (*aphar ha-adamah*) points, then, to the presiding principle according to which the elementary particles or atoms of earthly substance are by nature "predisposed" to take their place as constituent parts of man's body. *Adamah* is the tendency of the earth to take on human form. No compulsion, then, was acting on the atoms of *adamah* when they were summoned by YHVH ELOHIM from the "four corners of the world" (*Zohar* I, 205b) to form man. That summons was, rather, a fulfillment of their *own* impetus toward manhood (*adamah*). We may say that the word *adamah* points to the mystery of the formation (*yetzirah*) of man from the atoms of earthly substance; and further, that, as the "breath of life" penetrated man's form and reached as far as those constituent atoms, they quivered in ecstasy.

Once man's body had been formed, its enlivening and ensouling by the breath of life (*neshamah hachayim*)—making of it a living soul (*nephesh chayah*)—came from quite another source than that of the substance of the earth: it came from God. When the living breath of God was breathed into it, man's form, shaped from earthly substance, was filled with content of divine provenance. Man as a *living soul* is that which came to be at that time, still remains, and will endure for all time. Speaking from the tradition of the Kabbalah, Rabbi Isaac says, concerning the nature of man:

> Observe that when the Holy One, blessed be He, created Adam, He gathered his earthly matter from the four corners of the world and fashioned him therefrom on the site of the Temple here below and drew to him a soul of life out of the Temple on high. Now, the soul is a compound of three grades, and hence it has three names, to wit, *nephesh* (vital principle), *ruach* (spirit), and *neshamah* (soul proper). *Nephesh* is the lowest of the three, *ruach* a grade higher, and *neshamah* the highest of all, dominating the others. These three grades are harmoniously combined in those men who have the good fortune to render service to their Master. For at first man possesses *nephesh*, which is a holy preparative for a higher stage. After he has achieved purity in the grade of *nephesh*, he is deemed fit to be crowned by the holy grade resting upon it, namely *ruach*. When he has

thus attained to the indwelling of *nephesh* and *ruach*, and qualified himself for worship of his Master in the requisite manner, the *neshamah*—the holy superior grade that dominates all the others—takes up its abode with him and crowns him, so that he becomes complete and perfected on all sides. . . .

Observe that *nephesh*, *ruach*, and *neshamah* are ascending grades. The lowest of them, *nephesh*, has its source in the perennial celestial stream; but it cannot exist permanently save with the help of *ruach*, which abides between fire and water. *Ruach* in its turn is sustained by *neshamah*, the higher grade above it, which is thus the source of both *nephesh* and *ruach*. As *ruach* receives its sustenance from *neshamah*, *nephesh* receives it in turn from *ruach*, so that the three form a unity.[1]

This teaching concerning man's nature is even more clearly expressed in another passage from the *Zohar*, where Rabbi Simeon communicates the following to his son Rabbi Eleazar and his comrades Rabbi Abba and Rabbi Judah:

"I marvel how indifferent men are to the words of the Torah and the problem of their own existence!" He proceeded to discourse on the text: *With my soul have I desired thee in the night, yea, with my spirit within me will I seek thee early.* (Isaiah 26:9) He said: "The inner meaning of this verse is as follows. When a man lies down in bed, his vital spirit (*nephesh*) leaves him and begins to mount on high, leaving with the body only the impression of a receptacle which contains the

---

[1] *Zohar* II, 205b–206a, trans. M. Simon and H. Sperling (New York: Soncino Press, 1984), 280–81.

heartbeat. The rest of it tries to soar from grade to grade, and in doing so it encounters certain bright but unclean essences. If it is pure and has not defiled itself by day, it rises above them; but if not, it becomes defiled among them and cleaves to them and does not rise any further. There they show her certain things which are going to happen in the near future; and sometimes they delude her and show her false things. Thus she goes about the whole night until the man wakes up, when she returns to her place. Happy are the righteous to whom God reveals His secrets in dreams, so that they may be on their guard against sin! Woe to the sinners who defile their bodies and their souls! As for those who have not defiled themselves during the day, when they fall asleep at night their souls begin to ascend, and first enter these grades which we have mentioned, but they do not cleave to them, and continue to mount further. The soul which is privileged thus to rise finally appears before the gate of the celestial palace, and yearns with all its might to behold the beauty of the King and to visit His sanctuary. This is the man who ever hath a portion in the world to come, and this is the soul whose yearning, when she ascends, is for the Holy One, blessed be He, and who does not cleave to those other bright essences, but seeks out the holy essence in the place from which she originally issued. Therefore, it is written, 'With my soul have I desired thee in the night,' to pursue after thee and not to be enticed away after false powers. Again, the words 'With my soul have I desired thee in the night' refer to the soul (*nephesh*) which has sway by night, while the words 'with my spirit within me will I seek thee early' refer to the spirit (*ruach*) which has sway by day. 'Soul' (*nephesh*) and 'spirit' (*ruach*) are not two separate grades, but one grade with two aspects. There is still a third aspect which should dominate these two and cleave to them as they to it, and which is called 'higher spirit' (*neshamah*). . . . This spirit enters into them and they cleave to it, and when it dominates, such a man is called holy, perfect, wholly devoted to God. 'Soul' (*nephesh*) is the lowest stirring, it supports and feeds the body and is closely connected with it. When it sufficiently qualifies itself, it becomes the throne on which rests the lower spirit (*ruach*), as it is written, 'until the spirit be poured on us from on high' (Isaiah 32:15). When both have prepared themselves sufficiently, they are qualified to receive the higher spirit (*neshamah*), to which the lower spirit (*ruach*) becomes a throne, and which is undiscoverable, supreme over all. Thus there is throne resting on throne, and a throne for the highest. . . . For *nephesh* is the lowest stirring to which the body cleaves, like the dark light at the bottom of the candle flame which clings to the wick and exists only through it. When fully kindled, it becomes a throne for the white light above it. When both are fully kindled, the white light becomes a throne for a light which cannot be fully discerned—an unknown something resting on that white light, and so there is formed a complete light."[2]

---

[2] *Zohar* I, 83a–b, trans. M. Simon and H. Sperling (New York: Soncino Press, 1984), 277–78.

A short, clear summary of the thoughts and ideas that lived (and live on still) in the Jewish mystical tradition concerning *nephesh, ruach,* and *neshamah* is also given in the following discourse of Rabbi Isaac:

> Happy are the righteous in this world and in the next, because they are altogether holy. Their body (*kuph*) is holy, their soul (*nephesh*) is holy, their spirit (*ruach*) is holy, their super-soul (*neshamah*) is holy of holies. These are three grades indissolubly united. If a man does well with his soul (*nephesh*), there descends upon him a certain crown called spirit (*ruach*), which stirs him to a deeper contemplation of the laws of the Holy King. If he does well with this spirit (*ruach*), he is invested with a noble holy crown called super-soul (*neshamah*), which can contemplate all.[3]

⊕

Returning to our main theme of the mystery of the breath, it should be remembered that the "breath of life" (*spiraculum vitae* in the translation of St. Jerome; *neshamah hachayim* in the Hebrew text of Genesis 2:7) is what is *highest* in man. It proceeds from God, and is the true, essential kernel of man. As may be seen from the original biblical text and also from the *Zohar* commentaries quoted above, the "breath of life" is the ultimate source, foundation, and primal cause of *every* aspect of our life: our organic-physical life; our psycho-corporeal life; and both our soul-spiritual and divine-spiritual life. One *single* life,

---

[3] *Zohar* V, 70, trans. M. Simon and H. Sperling (New York: Soncino Press, 1984), 67.

which is to say, the "breath of life" (*neshamah hachayim*), comes to expression in us on quite different levels: in our corporeal breathing and heartbeat; in our thinking and mental picturing (or inner representations);[4] and in our praying and meditating.

To be very clear: just as our breathing and heartbeat are expressions of the "breath of life" in the waking and sleeping conditions of the *body*, so may our thinking and mental picturing be likened to the breathing and heartbeat of the *spirit*, and, likewise, our praying and meditating to the breathing and heartbeat of our true or divine *self* (or *atma* in Hindu philosophy). Above and beyond these expressions of the "breath of life" stands God Himself, of course, as origin and source.

The being or substance of man's true self, then, is the "breath of life" (*neshamah hachayim*) breathed out by God. This breath of God is the breath of love, of divine love, which is both the primal source, and the very being, of the living soul. If this "breath of life" should descend to the level of spirit (*ruach*), it becomes striving for truth, which is no other than that "breath of life" expressed through thinking and inner picturing or representation. If this "breath of life" should descend further to the life of our psycho-corporeal constitution (*nephesh*), it becomes the author of health as expressed in the harmonious concord between the psychic and life functions of the body. Nowadays one would say, rather, that it brings about psycho-corporeal "parallelism" (which is in fact the exact meaning of *nephesh*). From this we see that the sequence or gradation *neshamah*, *ruach*, *nephesh* signifies the "actuality" of love, truth, and health.

---

[4] *Vorstellen.*

The "breath of life" (*neshamah*) is the root and reason of religious life; the spirit (*ruach*) is the root and reason of striving after wisdom; and the combined principles of incorporating psychic aspects in bodily functions and bodily aspects in psychic functions (*nephesh*) constitutes the root and reason of our incarnated life on earth. Love, wisdom, and health arise, then, through the activity of one single stream of life, whose source is love. It is the "breath of love" breathed out by God that makes of the life present in man a *living soul.*

From the very beginning, man was created as a bearer of love. He is not *homo sapiens* only, but, beyond that, *homo amans.* In this sense, we may say that the biblical account of man's genesis as a living soul through the divine "breath of life" is recapitulated in the First Letter of John: "God is love, and he who abides in love abides in God, and God abides in him." (1 John 4:16)

⊕

Life is breathing, and of this there are two kinds: the breathing of air, which effects the physically necessary penetration of the blood with oxygen, ozone, and the life-element or *prana* (as it is designated in Sanskrit)—all of which are necessary for life; and inner soul-breathing, which through prayer and meditation breathes God, just as the body breathes air. The first breathing is that of health, the second that of religion. Just as we need to breathe air for our physical life, so do we need—through religious prayer and meditation—to breathe God for our soul life. The primal religion of mankind (*religio naturalis*) is rooted in the "breath of life" spoken of in the Bible, which never ceases, and will never cease, for it is eternal.

The German theologian and philosopher Friedrich Schleiermacher held that religion derives from mankind's "feeling of absolute dependence." This feeling, which is actually that of having been breathed out by God, is in truth the primal, most universal human experience of the reality of God. For man's soul, it is the primary "proof of God."

⊕

In the beginning, breathing was very different from what it has since become. It was a holism of *horizontal* inbreathing and outbreathing of air (along with the "vitality" of *prana* or life-force contained within it) and *vertical* breathing of prayer and meditation, divine worship and praise, union with God, understanding of and insight into the divine. Primordial (or, holistic) breathing was thereby engaged with the eternal through all three soul faculties of thinking, feeling, and willing. The memory of this primordial breathing lives on in the Hindu practice of yoga, but it lives on equally in the Eastern Orthodox Christian practice of the "Jesus prayer": "Lord Jesus Christ, Son of God, have mercy on me, a sinner." These words are repeated over and over until they take on a life of their own—in synchronization with the breathing and the beating of the heart—to the point that they come to be prayed unceasingly, day and night, together with the breath and heartbeat. It is thus that the apostle Paul's injunction to "pray without ceasing" (1 Thessalonians 5:17) can be fulfilled.

The primordial holism of breathing corresponded to the primordial holism of *speech*, which is no other than breathing formed into sounds. The loss of the single, universal language reported in the Bible (Genesis 11:9) as the confusion of tongues that followed in the wake of the building of the Tower of Babel, marked as well the disappearance of the primordial holism of breathing, which became instead individual and arbitrary. As a polar analogue to this, the Pentecost miracle marked the resurrection both of the primordial breathing and of the primordial language of mankind. The apostles were thereby enabled to speak again a single, universal language—one that was understood by people of different lands as though it were their native tongue.

As we have said, the primordial language spoken before the building of the Tower of Babel was as much a holism as was the primordial breathing. It was, thus, more an immediate transference of thought than a means of conveying information; that is, it was directed more at awakening intuition and understanding than at offering *explanations*. It offered *intimations*. But there was no need to "explain" these intimations, because they were not in the least ambiguous or indefinite. They were more like beams of light, or lightning flashes, fully coincident with the lucidity of their own intuitional content. Both speaker and listener participated *equally* in this lucidity. It was a matter of the depths of the speaker's heart penetrating to the depths of the listener's heart: a kind of "cordiality" or "heart magic."[5] But again, as a polar analogue, this was the case as well with the later "speaking in tongues" of the apostles and disciples at Pentecost, which, regardless of their country of origin, was experienced by those present as their mother tongue. But of course! What could be closer to each person than the language of the depths of their heart?

---

[5] *Herzlichkeit.*

⊕

Concentration. The gift of feeling one's way into things and penetrating them with insight presupposes the ability to concentrate. This ability is often presented as the result of a kind of mental gymnastic. Since the contents of ordinary associative thinking are by nature quite involuntary (arising "of themselves" in such a way as to divert and scatter our attention), one such exercise is to combat this tendency by forcefully and repeatedly concentrating on a freely chosen object. This exercise imposes limits on the spontaneous scripting of our mental life by associative thinking, and in due course is meant to bring it to a standstill.

The opening sentence of Patanjali's *Yoga Sutras* (the classic work on yoga) is "yoga is the suppression of the automatic movement of the thought substance" (*Yoga citta vritti nirodha*). European yoga practitioners put this precept into practice by paying close attention to the point where a vagrant thought first appears during their contemplation, and then reversing the spontaneous sequence of associations that led to its appearance, tracing it back to its origin and thereby laying it to rest. Such is the method employed to accomplish "the suppression of the automatic movement of the thought substance" mentioned by Patanjali. But then, as a means of preventing his attention from being diverted in the first place, the aspirant must *also* practice focusing on a specially chosen object with the intention of holding it (and nothing else) in consciousness. In practice, however, this exercise is often done in an artificially forced way.

This gives us occasion to ask what, in the truest sense, the faculty of concentration actually is. One thing it is *not*, is the outcome of desperately fixing our inner gaze on a single object—just as it is *not* (as we have seen) the outcome of obsessively exhausting ourselves fending off clandestine onslaughts of association. So again, what exactly *is* the faculty of concentration? It is the sequel to or outcome of the inner peace and stillness of "living into" a single object in a kind of *breathing*. It is an expression of the condition of inner peace, of the stillness of our soul life, extending its effect even as far as the breath, so that breathing becomes as deep and as peaceful as is the soul when concentrated in a state of poised inner stillness. True concentration is not a condition of fretful, strained attention, but one of relaxation—expressed in deep, peaceful breathing. The psychosomatic key to the gift of concentration is the breathing; in the final analysis, everything depends on this.

Despite what has just been said, however, it would be a mistake to believe that exercises to control and master *breathing* should come before exercises to master concentration. For in fact, such exercises as breathing air in for a certain number of seconds, holding it for some seconds, breathing it out again at a given rate, and then holding the lungs empty of air for a set span, can actually lead to a *negative* outcome. Though frequently recommended in yoga manuals, this practice often results in giving over the natural, autonomous regulation of the breath to mentally-commandeered respiration, with the result that the practitioner may experience unpleasant (and even dangerous) attacks of asphyxiation during sleep.

To develop the faculty of concentration, we do not need to control and regulate the breath in accordance with some arbitrary regimen. We need only cultivate a manner of breathing that mirrors the peace and quiet of the condition of the soul when unsullied by intentional and arbitrary mental interference. During concentration, then, breathing becomes as regular and natural, as free and autonomous, as it is during sleep—but with the difference, of course, that by "sleep" we mean here an "enhanced wakefulness."

A pure conscience, and love of nature and of our fellow-men, contributes more toward the attainment of concentration than any contrived praxis of breathing exercises could ever do.

⊕

Breathing is not limited, however, to the role of mirroring the *soul* in its various states. It can also be spiritualized; that is, elevated to mirroring the *spirit* transcending the soul (*ruach* in the sense of the above-cited teaching of the *Zohar*). But that is not all: it can be elevated even further. It can rise above mirroring the spirit to mirroring the true and immortal *self*. This is the "breath of life," the *neshamah*, of which the Bible and the *Zohar* speak. In the *neshamah*, the breath becomes an organ for harmonizing with, or participating in, the divine breath itself.

Now, the divine breath—this "breath of life"—is nothing other than the eternal coming-into-being from God of the very kernel of man. God is eternal Being, and man's true self is nothing other than the "breath of life" that is eternally coming into being from eternal Being, and thus resting eternally in the being-bestowing breath of the Godhead.

When breathing reaches this uttermost degree of inwardness, the experience of our true self thus begotten is as a star in the heaven of God's eternal Being. This experience of the being-bestowing breath of God brings with it also complete *certainty* concerning God and immortality. For faith is not simply a matter of holding something to be true, but of *experiencing its truth* in the being-bestowing breath of the eternal God. The experience of the breath of eternity, felt deep in the life of the soul, is the root and source of religion—of *all* religions. Belief in God and immortality is more than holding these things to be true, for what we mean by "holding to be true" is in essence nothing other than our recognition of and *assent* to the experience of certainty we feel in the depths of our soul—and which we affirm with a resounding "Yes!"

This way of understanding the origin of religion and of belief in God has precious little chance, however, of being taken seriously in today's world—with the possible exception of Jungian depth psychology and Platonic philosophy. For Jungian research is alone in having concluded that in the depths of our souls we are religious beings; and Platonic philosophy is alone in doing justice to the fact that there is a non-empirical way to attain certainty concerning God and immortality, a way based upon "vertical memory"— which is to say, based upon the recognition that we may come to *direct experience* of our higher self *within* the self (or, "I") of our ordinary waking consciousness.

Now, there are three experiences accessible to each of us without exception that may in a natural-supernatural way impress upon our quietened, stilled souls something of the breath of eternity we are speaking of. These are experiences that recall to our awareness *the breathing of the higher self in the heaven of the eternal Being of the Trinity.* By this we mean an inner breathing in connection with the experience of *night,* of *sunset,* and of *sunrise.*

V

Natural & Supernatural Images of the Holy Trinity
Three Meditations

The Message of the Night Sky

O THE SOUL GROWN QUIET AND STILL, THE starry night sky testifies to the silent majesty of the kingdom of eternal Being that lies beyond the province of birth and death, of becoming and passing away. The solemn majesty of the starry heavens proclaims the all-pervading presence of the divine Being upon which all the universe is founded. It is as though the world of becoming and passing away were caught up and pressed to the bosom of eternal Being in an all-encompassing embrace. In the starry night sky, eternal Being draws so near to the becomings and passings-away of existence that we may well wonder how we ever failed to mark this great peace and stillness (which undergirds all the multiplicity of existence) also during the brightness of day!

We sense the presence of the eternal within the temporal—of which the starry night sky speaks—as all-embracing, all-permeating holiness. In truth, what is holiness but a perception of the presence of eternal Being in the temporal world? The soul that perceives this presence knows with certainty that this holiness has always been, and is still, experienced in all its duly portioned degrees of intensity by the blessed incorporeal spirits of the cosmos: angels, archangels, principalities, powers, virtues, dominions, thrones, cherubim, and seraphim. And as we contemplate our own due portion of this "breathing together" with the starry night sky, we come ineluctably to comprehend the perfect expression of this experience in the closing acclamation of the prefatory of the Mass, where we hear that:

> the cherubim and seraphim who day and night never cease to sing: "Holy, holy, holy Lord, God of power and might, heaven and earth are full of your glory. Hosanna in the highest. Blessed is he who comes in the name of the Lord. Hosanna in the highest."

The thrice-repeated "holy" of this acclamation is not solely a measure of high regard; it is, rather, *the breath of the presence of eternal Being*, sighing through the temporal world. It is the heavenly hierarchies' awareness of the presence of eternal Being—the awareness, that is, of those very beings who share in eternal Being. It is this eternal Being, the "God of power and might"—root and source of all selfhood—Who is recognized and acknowledged by all beings that are endowed with selfhood, when, with one voice (*una voce*), they sing:

> Holy, holy, holy Lord, God of power and might, heaven and earth are full of your glory. Hosanna in the highest.

Is it conceivable that any being who experiences its true self as apportioned by due degree among the eternal celestial hierarchies (whether man, angel, or other choir) could fail to join in this heavenly acclamation? Surely not, for this

68

chorus acknowledges the highest conceivable good, the highest conceivable gift, that there could ever be in all the universe—namely, the bestowal of being (together with an endless horizon of possibilities for its further unfolding) by the Bestower of Being Himself, God the *Father*.

Thus does the starry night sky speak of the reality of the Father God to the soul that, having grown inwardly quiet and still, breathes the Deep.

⊕

The Message of Sunset

Even as the starry night sky instills the breathing soul with the all-pervading presence of eternal Being and the holiness of the Bestower of Being—of the Father—so does the experience of sunset proclaim the descent of the *Son* from the heaven of eternal Being *into the realm of existence,* the realm of birth and death. The glorious colors of the sunset need not be wondered at solely for their vibrant beauty, for in truth that beauty is but a supernal likeness and symbol for the unutterable beauty of the Son's love-sacrifice that stands behind it. The setting sun tells the story of the Son's leave-taking from the kingdom of eternal Being in order to incarnate in the world of temporal existence, the realm of birth and death. In the words of the Creed:

> He came down from heaven: by the power of the
> Holy Spirit he became incarnate from the Virgin
> Mary, and was made man.
>
> *Descendit de coelo et incarnatus est de Spiritu sancto ex Maria virgine et homo factus est.*

But the setting sun mirrors *more than this.* It mirrors as well the unutterable beauty of Jesus Christ's love-sacrifice in his *later* leave-taking from his disciples, just before his sufferings and sacrificial death on Golgotha. Yes, the sunset proclaims *both* the Son's leave-taking from the kingdom of the Father in heaven *prior* to his Incarnation, and its *later* reflection when, at the Last Supper, he took leave of his disciples. The "theme" of Christ's leave-taking from the Father is reprised when we meditate on his farewell discourses in John's gospel (John 14–17). What the soul experiences at sunset is akin to what the farewell discourses of John's gospel evoke. When these discourses are read and meditated upon, we experience anew the heavenly mystery of the sunset of Christ's departure from the Father on his path into earthly incarnation.

Is it not this same twofold experience of leave-taking that, for example, indigenous Mexican laborers and vaqueros daily wait upon as they linger in the silence of the setting sun—which for them is a life necessity? It is well-known among plantation owners and ranchers that the time of dusk must be set aside for their laborers so that they may contemplate the sunset's beauty ("beauty" meant here in more than an aesthetic sense). Do we not feel in the sunset the *same* beauty that we feel in the love-sacrifice of the Son of God as reported in the farewell discourses of John's gospel? Is not the feeling experienced at sunset by so-called "natural souls" a longing for absolute beauty—a beauty without which such souls know in their hearts they cannot truly live?

We cannot help but think here of St. Augustine's words: *anima humana naturaliter christiana* ("the natural constitution of the human soul is Christian"). Only in light of these words can we understand that every soul living close to nature feels the need to experience and to contemplate the sunset. For in truth, this contemplation opens out upon the unspeakable beauty of the Son of God, who took leave of the heaven of eternal Being to become incarnate in the realm of birth and death; and who later, as the God-Man Jesus Christ, took leave of human life to embrace sacrificial death. Neither in heaven, nor on earth, can anything so beautiful and so moving be found as the descent of the Son of God from the heaven of eternal Being, and then, later, his leave-taking as the God-Man just before his Passion and

Death upon the Cross. It is this same beauty that takes hold of "natural souls" and fills them.

A soul that truly *is* a soul cannot help but be deeply moved by the beauty of the Son of God. This is exactly what St. Augustine meant when he wrote: "the natural constitution of the human soul is Christian." Were this not so, how could we make sense of the leave-taking mandate given the apostles to "go therefore and make disciples of all nations, baptizing them in the name of the Father and of the Son and of the Holy Spirit"? (Matthew 28:19) Even as bread and water presuppose (and stand ready to *still*) hunger and thirst, so does the working of grace and revelation presuppose (and stand ready to *satisfy*) the yearnings and questioning concerns that come to expression in the need to bear witness with hushed emotion to the sun at its setting.

It would be both facile and false, however, to infer from the fact that such people quite naturally and soulfully inbreathe the mystery of the sunset (which lies so close to their hearts) that "for all the more reason" people with such sensitivities *must* also be found among "civilized" European Christians. This is simply not so. In Europe there have been (and still are) periods during which the true life of the soul of entire peoples has been (and still is) in grave danger of withering away. This holds true not only of the tidal wave of materialism that flooded Europe, both East and West, during the twentieth century, but also of the outpourings of the Enlightenment during the age of rationalism in the eighteenth century, which in the first place paved the way for that materialism.

The danger that was facing mankind at that juncture was so great that, in order to avert it, a preventive intercession proved necessary. This took place in the second half of the seventeenth century with the revelation of the most Sacred Heart of Jesus. This revelation led to the cult of devotion to the most Sacred Heart of Jesus, which spread rapidly in Catholic countries and took firm hold there. Devotion to the Sacred Heart of Jesus was meant to save the soul of mankind, for the danger breaking in upon it during the time of the Enlightenment threatened to turn man into a "centaur," a creature of only head and limbs, of reason and will—a clever enough beast, but lacking heart or soul. The mission of the cult of devotion to the Sacred Heart of Jesus was meant to rekindle the heart and thereby set the light, warmth, and life streaming from the Heart of Jesus against the will to power, as also against the rationalism at its beck and call.

The soul's survival—understood as the refining and deepening of the heart's life—can by no means be taken as a given. And souls operating under the aegis of "civilized" Christian humanity are (as mentioned before) no exception. All manner of danger threatens to destroy the human soul. This is why it was so important during the Enlightenment (and remains so in our day) to nurture, encourage, and stimulate the life of the soul with the help of devotion to the Sacred Heart of Jesus.

Finally, rounding out our point, we may say that the very same moral depth and beauty that is so stirring to witness and experience through devotion to the Sacred Heart of Jesus is witnessed and experienced as well by "natural" souls (such as we have mentioned) when at close of day in deepest contemplation they behold the sunset. For the deepest essence of the experience of the setting of the true Sun is in truth the Being of the most Sacred Heart of Jesus—the

Sun, as it were, of all hearts—which is, as the *Litany of the Sacred Heart* tells us, *Cor Jesu, Rex et centrum omnium cordium* ("Heart of Jesus, King and center of all hearts").

⊕

The Message of Sunrise

Sunrise, the birth of the new day, is the awe-inspiring event of the awakening of manifold beings heretofore sunk in sleep and forgetfulness. But what is "awakening"? It is the re-illumining of the past through memory and the resurrection of hope in the future.

The essence of the power that awakens, that overcomes sleep and forgetting, is *hope*. Every dawning of a new day, every awakening, is accomplished by the power of hope, which suffuses all mankind, and the beings of nature also. The birds' dawn-chorus greeting each new day tells us that, upon waking, the beings of nature are filled with hope.

The manuscript ends here

⊕

Biographical Afterword

ALENTIN TOMBERG WAS BORN ON FEBRUARY 27, 1900, the second son of a senior civil servant in St. Petersburg. There he attended a classical high school and took three semesters of history and philosophy. Although brought up as a Protestant, he also came into early contact with the intellectual world of Russian Orthodoxy and with Theosophical ideas. The happy years of his youth were brought to an end by the Russian Revolution. With his parents and his brother, he went into exile in Estonia, where he at first made ends meet as an agricultural worker, a pharmacist, an artist, and a teacher. At that time he also studied comparative religion at the University of Tartu, as well as several ancient and modern languages, laying down the bases of his broad and deep learning. From 1924 onwards, a post as an official in the head office of the Estonian Postal Service freed him from material worries, and later enabled him to acquire a small *dacha* near Tallinn. In those years he became so deeply and convincingly versed in the work of Rudolf Steiner that the German-speaking branch of the Estonian Anthroposophical Society chose him, at the age of twenty-five, as their chairman. He often regretted that he had never met Steiner (who died in 1925) in person.

From 1930 onwards, Tomberg published numerous essays in anthroposophical journals. Between 1933 and 1938, his most important anthroposophical work appeared in typescript: twelve meditations each on the Old and New Testaments.[1] In the same years he composed works on Rudolf Steiner's Foundation Stone Meditation, on the appearance of Christ in the etheric world, and on the inner development of the human being. Above all it was his concern, in ever new ways, to move Christ into the center of Anthroposophy, to awaken and deepen love for Christ, and to understand Christ's life on earth, his death, and finally his resurrection, as the turning-point of world history, so as to find a path toward moral answerability to the triune God. Many who listened to him at that time relate how infinitely they were indebted to him.

Yet the official Anthroposophical Society saw its first task as limited to looking after and extending Rudolf Steiner's legacy, and in consequence, Dutch friends invited him to the Netherlands, making it a second homeland for him. But when the chairman of the Dutch Anthroposophical Society asked that Tomberg withdraw, he did so—although never, certainly, from Rudolf Steiner himself, to whom he always remained connected by a most inward spiritual fellowship.

In the years of World War II and the German occupation, Tomberg was in hiding from the Nazis in Amsterdam, where he lived on the proceeds of private language tuition. He was surrounded by a small circle of loyal friends, whom he led ever deeper into the mysteries of Christianity in an extended course on the Our Father prayer. In those years he joined a congregation of the Orthodox Church.[2] But about the time the War ended, Tomberg had arrived at a decision:

---

[1] Twelve further meditations on the Apocalypse (and thus on the future of humanity) were given as lectures by Tomberg, but only three of them were published, after which Tomberg stopped working on them.

[2] He had been a member of the Orthodox Church since around 1930.

in an internment camp for displaced persons (where he was assisting) he entered the Roman Catholic Church.[3]

Tomberg regarded it an error with serious consequences only ever to see the Catholic Church as an institution that wanted to make up the mind of its members for them, to deprive them of intellectual freedom, or even as the institution of the Inquisition and of religious persecution. For him, this would be to confuse the Church with the *doppelgänger* or "egregore" that accompanies every institution. Tomberg had learned to distinguish the true and authentic Church from such "doubles," and to love that Church. And he possessed the fair-mindedness to acknowledge that this true Church had, even from an external point of view, stepped forward in face of the suffering and challenges it had had to suffer at the hands of National Socialism.

The roots of Tomberg's conversion lay, not in personal motives, but in his love for Christ and in his sense of responsibility to the world. Many of Tomberg's previous friends wondered whether such a great spirit would not be giving up his freedom by fitting in with the Church. But Tomberg's own experience did not confirm these fears on his friends' part. He understood intellectual freedom to mean the opening up of the human being to what was objectively good and true (without permitting this to be colored in any way by subjective sympathy or antipathy), and the incorporation of this objectively good and true into his eternal self. In this sense, Tomberg was able to retain his freedom and identity even as a Catholic. For the core of what had turned out to be truth according to Tomberg's

---

[3] He was, however, allowed to receive communion in the Orthodox Church as well.

own insight was precisely the message that the Church brings into the world as a whole, and that the Church serves by handing down the mysteries transmitted from generation to generation, by administering the sacraments, by celebrating the liturgical year, by preaching and bestowing blessings, and by turning towards the very simplest people across the world without the least arrogance. The educated and the uneducated alike join here in adoration of the threefold God, in worship of what is holy, in the singing of Christmas carols (which Tomberg so deeply loved). For anyone seriously enquiring after the truth about the deeper reasons for Tomberg's conversion, it shines forth with ample clarity from his work.

In the years after the War, Tomberg gave lectures in several cities in the Rhineland. Those in the audience at these earlier lectures recollect with great enthusiasm how he explained, among other things, the deeper meaning of the rosary. Alongside this, Tomberg also addressed the political realities of the Nazi period in several jurisprudential writings, including: *Degeneration und Regeneration der Rechtswissenschaften,*[4] and *Grundlagen des Völkerrechts als Menschheitsrecht.*[5] For the former work, the Faculty of Law at the University of Cologne awarded him a doctorate. During this period he was given responsibility in the city of Mülheim, in the Ruhr region, for rebuilding the adult education center.

---

[4] Published in English as *The Art of the Good: On the Regeneration of Fallen Justice* (Brooklyn, NY: Angelico Press, 2021).

[5] *The Fundamental Principles of International Law as a Law of Humanity.* English translation in preparation by Angelico Press.

In 1948, English friends obtained a position for Tomberg at the BBC, in which he was assisted not only by his knowledge of languages, but also by his political perspective and judgment. At first he lived in London, then in a small house in a leafy suburb of Reading (a city on the Thames, where he was able to use the local university library for his research work in the evenings). He took his pension at the earliest opportunity, to wholly devote himself to his writing. Tomberg's Polish-French wife Maria was not only an understanding fellow traveler but in many respects a congenial collaborator with him. The deep spiritual fellowship they shared was a continual source of human happiness to Tomberg in a life marked by an absence of recognition, and by isolation.

⊕

A word on my own meeting with Valentin Tomberg, whom I for a long time tried, as an anthroposophist and Catholic, to meet, but without success, and whom I finally met in very unusual circumstances. I had discovered that he was a friend of the retired Cologne professor of jurisprudence, Ernst von Hippel, and that von Hippel might perhaps be able to introduce me to Tomberg. But I had been unable to make von Hippel's acquaintance until, surprisingly, I was summoned to take over his former professorial position! That is how I was introduced to Tomberg.

In the last years of his life, Tomberg was not only a teacher to me, but also a fatherly, and incredibly warm and caring, friend. In his conversation, deep seriousness alternated with relaxed cheerfulness, wit, and humor. I never found him to be anything but kind, honest, fair-minded, and clear with his whole being. Every meeting, every letter,

indeed every phone call, had something refreshing, invigo-
rating, and regenerating in it.

From my knowledge of his life and thought I should
only like to add two points. His "social" activity consisted
above all in the attempt, through extensive daily and
nightly prayer, to bring practical help to many of the dead
in purgatory. Over and over again, he emphasized that it
was of particular importance not to think of heaven as an
abstract principle. It was, rather, to be understood as the
divine milieu, both of the presence of angels filled with
concrete life, and of other personal beings—beings who
have a name, who have qualities, who work and suffer, and
who participate in the great drama of world history. He
spoke mostly of God as the Father; of God's Son as the
Master. He wished to be completely obedient to them.

⊕

During a visit at Christmas in 1972, Tomberg brought me
various manuscripts, among which was the one published
here, as well as spiritual journals and other sketches, and
appointed me executor of his literary estate. It was as
though, despite being healthy, he had an intimation of his
imminent death; in any event, it was to be our last meeting.
A few weeks later he had a stroke. He died on February 24,
1973. Death also overtook his wife a short time afterwards,
as he had once with great definiteness predicted to me
when I was asking him about his plans for his old age. I was
to publish this, and the other three manuscripts delivered
to me at that time, when the time was right, which, he had
said, "would not be the case before ten years had elapsed."

As regards certain passages standing, perhaps, in need of
explicit elucidation, I ask readers not to withdraw their

trust from Tomberg, even where they might have skeptical questions. From my own experience, I can assure such readers of two things. First, it was more important to Tomberg to respect the intellectual and moral freedom of others than to convince them, and he always took the other person's misgivings and objections seriously. Second, questions often occasioned his giving explicit answers that made it possible to see in a new light what had been stumbling-blocks, and made them surprisingly comprehensible.

MARTIN KRIELE
Cologne, Whitsun, 1985

9 781621 388371